Math for Machine Learning
Open Doors to Data Science and Artificial Intelligence

Richard Han

2 Linear Regression
3 Discriminant Analysis
4 Logistic Regression
[5. Neural Networks
[6. maximum marginal Class
[7. Support vector classifier
[8. SVM-classifier

CONTENTS

PREFACE

Welcome to Math for Machine Learning: Open Doors to Data Science and Artificial Intelligence. This is a first textbook in math for machine learning. Be sure to get the companion online course Math for Machine Learning here: <u>Math for Machine Learning Online Course</u>. The online course can be very helpful in conjunction with this book.

The prerequisites for this book and the online course are Linear Algebra, Multivariable Calculus, and Probability. You can find my online course on Linear Algebra here: <u>Linear Algebra Course</u>.

We will not do any programming in this book.

This book will get you started in machine learning in a smooth and natural way, preparing you for more advanced topics and dispelling the belief that machine learning is complicated, difficult, and intimidating.

I want you to succeed and prosper in your career, life, and future endeavors. I am here for you. Visit me at: <u>Online Math Training</u>

1 - INTRODUCTION

Welcome to Math for Machine Learning: Open Doors to Data Science and Artificial Intelligence! My name is Richard Han. This is a first textbook in math for machine learning.

Ideal student:

If you're a working professional needing a refresher on machine learning or a complete beginner who needs to learn Machine Learning for the first time, this book is for you. If your busy schedule doesn't allow you to go back to a traditional school, this book allows you to study on your own schedule and further your career goals without being left behind.

If you plan on taking machine learning in college, this is a great way to get ahead.

If you're currently struggling with machine learning or have struggled with it in the past, now is the time to master it.

Benefits of studying this book:

After reading this book, you will have refreshed your knowledge of machine learning for your career so that you can earn a higher salary.

You will have a required prerequisite for lucrative career fields such as Data Science and Artificial Intelligence.

You will be in a better position to pursue a masters or PhD degree in machine learning and data science.

Why Machine Learning is important:

- Famous uses of machine learning include:
  - Linear discriminant analysis. Linear discriminant analysis can be used to solve classification problems such as spam filtering and classifying patient illnesses.

- o Logistic regression. Logistic regression can be used to solve binary classification problems such as determining whether a patient has a certain form of cancer or not.
- o Artificial neural networks. Artificial neural networks can be used for applications such as self-driving cars, recommender systems, online marketing, reading medical images, speech and face recognition
- o Support Vector machines. Real world applications of SVM's include classification of proteins and classification of images.

What my book offers:

In this book, I cover core topics such as:

- **Linear Regression**
- **Linear Discriminant Analysis**
- **Logistic Regression**
- **Artificial Neural Networks**
- **Support Vector Machines**

I explain each definition and go through each example step by step so that you understand each topic clearly. Throughout the book, there are practice problems for you to try. Detailed solutions are provided after each problem set.

I hope you benefit from the book.

Best regards,

Richard Han

2 – LINEAR REGRESSION

LINEAR REGRESSION

Suppose we have a set of data $(x_1, y_1), \ldots, (x_N, y_N)$. This is called the training data.

Each x_i is a vector $\begin{bmatrix} x_{i1} \\ x_{i2} \\ \vdots \\ x_{ip} \end{bmatrix}$ of measurements, where x_{i1} is an instance of the first input variable X_1, x_{i2} is an instance of the second input variable X_2, etc. $X_1, \ldots, X_p$ are called *features* or *predictors*.

$y_1, \ldots, y_N$ are instances of the output variable Y, which is called the *response*.

In linear regression, we assume that the response depends on the input variables in a linear fashion:

$y = f(X) + \varepsilon$, where $f(X) = \beta_0 + \beta_1 X_1 + \cdots + \beta_p X_p$.

Here, ε is called the *error term* and $\beta_0, \ldots, \beta_p$ are called *parameters*.

We don't know the values of $\beta_0, \ldots, \beta_p$. However, we can use the training data to approximate the values of $\beta_0, \ldots, \beta_p$. What we'll do is look at the amount by which the predicted value $f(x_i)$ differs from the actual y_i for each of the pairs $(x_1, y_1), \ldots, (x_N, y_N)$ from the training data. So we have $y_i - f(x_i)$ as the difference. We then square this and take the sum for $i = 1, \ldots, N$:

$$\sum_{i=1}^{N} \left(y_i - f(x_i) \right)^2$$

This is called the *residual sum of squares* and denoted $RSS(\beta)$ where $\beta = \begin{bmatrix} \beta_0 \\ \beta_1 \\ \vdots \\ \beta_p \end{bmatrix}$.

We want the residual sum of squares to be as small as possible. Essentially, this means that we want our predicted value $f(x_i)$ to be as close to the actual value y_i as possible, for each of the pairs (x_i, y_i). Doing this will give us a linear function of the input variables that best fits the given training data. In

MATH FOR MACHINE LEARNING

the case of only one input variable, we get the best fit line. In the case of two input variables, we get the best fit plane. And so on, for higher dimensions.

THE LEAST SQUARES METHOD

By minimizing $RSS(\beta)$, we can obtain estimates $\widehat{\beta_0}, \widehat{\beta_1}, ..., \widehat{\beta_p}$ of the parameters $\beta_0, ..., \beta_p$. This method is called the **least squares method**.

$$\text{Let } X = \begin{bmatrix} 1 & x_{11} & x_{12} & \cdots & x_{1p} \\ 1 & x_{21} & x_{22} & \cdots & x_{2p} \\ \vdots & & & & \\ 1 & x_{N1} & x_{N2} & \cdots & x_{Np} \end{bmatrix} \text{ and } \boldsymbol{y} = \begin{bmatrix} y_1 \\ \vdots \\ y_N \end{bmatrix}.$$

$$\text{Then } \boldsymbol{y} - X\beta = \begin{bmatrix} y_1 \\ \vdots \\ y_N \end{bmatrix} - \begin{bmatrix} 1 & x_{11} & x_{12} & \cdots & x_{1p} \\ 1 & x_{21} & x_{22} & \cdots & x_{2p} \\ \vdots & & & & \\ 1 & x_{N1} & x_{N2} & \cdots & x_{Np} \end{bmatrix} \begin{bmatrix} \beta_0 \\ \beta_1 \\ \vdots \\ \beta_p \end{bmatrix}$$

$$= \begin{bmatrix} y_1 \\ \vdots \\ y_N \end{bmatrix} - \begin{bmatrix} \beta_0 + \beta_1 x_{11} + \cdots + \beta_p x_{1p} \\ \beta_0 + \beta_1 x_{21} + \cdots + \beta_p x_{2p} \\ \vdots \\ \beta_0 + \beta_1 x_{N1} + \cdots + \beta_p x_{Np} \end{bmatrix}$$

$$= \begin{bmatrix} y_1 \\ \vdots \\ y_N \end{bmatrix} - \begin{bmatrix} f(x_1) \\ f(x_2) \\ \vdots \\ f(x_N) \end{bmatrix}$$

$$= \begin{bmatrix} y_1 - f(x_1) \\ \vdots \\ y_N - f(x_N) \end{bmatrix}$$

So $(\boldsymbol{y} - X\beta)^T(\boldsymbol{y} - X\beta) = \sum_{i=1}^{N}\left(y_i - f(x_i)\right)^2 = RSS(\beta)$

$\implies \quad RSS(\beta) = (\boldsymbol{y} - X\beta)^T(\boldsymbol{y} - X\beta).$

Consider the vector of partial derivatives of $RSS(\beta)$:

$$\begin{bmatrix} \dfrac{\partial RSS(\beta)}{\partial \beta_0} \\ \dfrac{\partial RSS(\beta)}{\partial \beta_1} \\ \vdots \\ \dfrac{\partial RSS(\beta)}{\partial \beta_p} \end{bmatrix}$$

$$RSS(\beta) = \left(y_1 - \left(\beta_0 + \beta_1 x_{11} + \cdots + \beta_p x_{1p}\right)\right)^2 + \cdots + \left(y_N - \left(\beta_0 + \beta_1 x_{N1} + \cdots + \beta_p x_{Np}\right)\right)^2$$

Let's take the partial derivative with respect to β_0.

$$\frac{\partial RSS(\beta)}{\partial \beta_0} = 2\left(y_1 - \left(\beta_0 + \beta_1 x_{11} + \cdots + \beta_p x_{1p}\right)\right) \cdot (-1) + \cdots + 2(y_N - (\beta_0 + \beta_1 x_{N1} + \cdots + \beta_p x_{Np})) \cdot (-1)$$

$$= -2 \cdot [1 \quad \cdots \quad 1](\boldsymbol{y} - X\beta)$$

Next, take the partial derivative with respect to β_1.

$$\frac{\partial RSS(\beta)}{\partial \beta_1} = 2\left(y_1 - \left(\beta_0 + \beta_1 x_{11} + \cdots + \beta_p x_{1p}\right)\right) \cdot (-x_{11}) + \cdots + 2(y_N - (\beta_0 + \beta_1 x_{N1} + \cdots + \beta_p x_{Np})) \cdot (-x_{N1})$$

$$= -2[x_{11} \quad \cdots \quad x_{N1}] \cdot (\boldsymbol{y} - X\beta)$$

In general, $\dfrac{\partial RSS(\beta)}{\partial \beta_k} = -2[x_{1k} \quad \cdots \quad x_{Nk}] \cdot (\boldsymbol{y} - X\beta)$

So,

$$\begin{bmatrix} \dfrac{\partial RSS(\beta)}{\partial \beta_0} \\ \dfrac{\partial RSS(\beta)}{\partial \beta_1} \\ \vdots \\ \dfrac{\partial RSS(\beta)}{\partial \beta_p} \end{bmatrix} = \begin{bmatrix} -2 \cdot [1 \quad \cdots \quad 1](\boldsymbol{y} - X\beta) \\ -2[x_{11} \quad \cdots \quad x_{N1}](\boldsymbol{y} - X\beta) \\ \vdots \\ -2[x_{1p} \quad \cdots \quad x_{Np}](\boldsymbol{y} - X\beta) \end{bmatrix}$$

$$= -2 \begin{bmatrix} 1 & \cdots & 1 \\ x_{11} & \cdots & x_{N1} \\ & \vdots & \\ x_{1p} & \cdots & x_{Np} \end{bmatrix} (\boldsymbol{y} - X\beta)$$

$$= -2X^T(\boldsymbol{y} - X\beta)$$

If we take the second derivative of $RSS(\beta)$, say $\dfrac{\partial^2 RSS(\beta)}{\partial \beta_k \partial \beta_j}$, we get

$$\frac{\partial}{\partial \beta_j}\left(2\left(y_1 - \left(\beta_0 + \beta_1 x_{11} + \cdots + \beta_p x_{1p}\right)\right) \cdot (-x_{1k}) + \cdots + 2\left(y_N - \left(\beta_0 + \beta_1 x_{N1} + \cdots + \beta_p x_{Np}\right)\right) \cdot (-x_{Nk})\right)$$

$$= 2x_{1j}x_{1k} + \cdots + 2x_{Nj}x_{Nk}$$

$$= 2(x_{1j}x_{1k} + \cdots + x_{Nj}x_{Nk})$$

Note $X = \begin{bmatrix} x_{10} & x_{11} & x_{12} & \cdots & x_{1p} \\ x_{20} & x_{21} & x_{22} & \cdots & x_{2p} \\ \vdots & & & & \\ x_{N0} & x_{N1} & x_{N2} & \cdots & x_{Np} \end{bmatrix}$

$\Rightarrow \qquad X^T X = \begin{bmatrix} x_{10} & x_{20} & \cdots & x_{N0} \\ x_{11} & x_{21} & \cdots & x_{N1} \\ \vdots & & & \\ x_{1p} & x_{2p} & \cdots & x_{Np} \end{bmatrix} \begin{bmatrix} x_{10} & x_{11} & \cdots & x_{1p} \\ x_{20} & x_{21} & \cdots & x_{2p} \\ \vdots & & & \\ x_{N0} & x_{N1} & \cdots & x_{Np} \end{bmatrix}$

$$= (a_{jk}) \qquad \text{where } a_{jk} = x_{1j}x_{1k} + \cdots + x_{Nj}x_{Nk}$$

So $\dfrac{\partial^2 RSS(\beta)}{\partial \beta_k \partial \beta_j} = 2a_{jk}$

$\Rightarrow$ The matrix of second derivatives of $RSS(\beta)$ is $2X^T X$. This matrix is called **the Hessian**. By the second derivative test, if the Hessian of $RSS(\beta)$ at a critical point is positive definite, then $RSS(\beta)$ has a local minimum there.

If we set our vector of derivatives to **0**, we get
$$-2X^T(\mathbf{y} - X\beta) = \mathbf{0}$$
$\Rightarrow \qquad -2X^T \mathbf{y} + 2X^T X\beta = \mathbf{0}$
$\Rightarrow \qquad 2X^T X\beta = 2X^T \mathbf{y}$
$\Rightarrow \qquad X^T X\beta = X^T \mathbf{y}$
$\Rightarrow \qquad \beta = (X^T X)^{-1} X^T \mathbf{y}.$

Thus, we solved for the vector of parameters $\begin{bmatrix} \beta_0 \\ \beta_1 \\ \vdots \\ \beta_p \end{bmatrix}$ which minimizes the residual sum of squares $RSS(\beta)$.

So we let $\begin{bmatrix} \widehat{\beta_0} \\ \widehat{\beta_1} \\ \vdots \\ \widehat{\beta_p} \end{bmatrix} = (X^T X)^{-1} X^T \mathbf{y}.$

LINEAR ALGEBRA SOLUTION TO LEAST SQUARES PROBLEM

We can arrive at the same solution for the least squares problem by using linear algebra.

Let $X = \begin{bmatrix} 1 & x_{11} & x_{12} & \cdots & x_{1p} \\ 1 & x_{21} & x_{22} & \cdots & x_{2p} \\ \vdots & & & & \\ 1 & x_{N1} & x_{N2} & \cdots & x_{Np} \end{bmatrix}$ and $\mathbf{y} = \begin{bmatrix} y_1 \\ \vdots \\ y_N \end{bmatrix}$ as before, from our training data. We want a

vector β such that $X\beta$ is close to $\mathbf{y}$. In other words, we want a vector β such that the distance $\|X\beta - \mathbf{y}\|$ between $X\beta$ and $\mathbf{y}$ is minimized. A vector β that minimizes $\|X\beta - \mathbf{y}\|$ is called a **least-squares solution** of $X\beta = y$.

X is an N by $(p + 1)$ matrix. We want a $\hat{\beta}$ in $\mathbb{R}^{p+1}$ such that $X\hat{\beta}$ is closest to y. Note that $X\hat{\beta}$ is a linear combination of the columns of X. So $X\hat{\beta}$ lies in the span of the columns of X, which is a subspace of $\mathbb{R}^N$ denoted $Col\ X$. So we want the vector in $Col\ X$ that is closest to y. The projection of y onto the subspace $Col\ X$ is that vector.

$proj_{Col\ X} y = X\hat{\beta}$ for some $\hat{\beta} \in \mathbb{R}^{p+1}$.

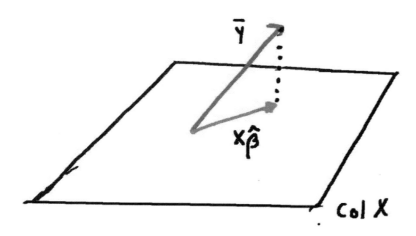

Consider $y - X\hat{\beta}$. Note that $y = X\hat{\beta} + (y - X\hat{\beta})$.

$\mathbb{R}^N$ can be broken into two subspaces $Col\ X$ and $(Col\ X)^\perp$, where $(Col\ X)^\perp$ is the subspace of $\mathbb{R}^N$ consisting of all vectors that are orthogonal to the vectors in $Col\ X$. Any vector in $\mathbb{R}^N$ can be written uniquely as $z + w$ where $z \in Col\ X$ and $w \in (Col\ X)^\perp$.

Since $y \in \mathbb{R}^N$, and $y = X\hat{\beta} + (y - X\hat{\beta})$, with $X\hat{\beta} \in Col\ X$, the second vector $y - X\hat{\beta}$ must lie in $(Col\ X)^\perp$.

$\implies$ $\quad y - X\hat{\beta}$ is orthogonal to the columns of X.

$\implies$ $\quad X^T(y - X\hat{\beta}) = 0$

$\implies$ $\quad X^T y - X^T X\hat{\beta} = 0.$

$\implies$ $\quad X^T X\hat{\beta} = X^T y.$

Thus, it turns out that the set of least-squares solutions of $X\beta = y$ consists of all and only the solutions to the matrix equation $X^T X\beta = X^T y$.

If $X^T X$ is positive definite, then the eigenvalues of $X^T X$ are all positive. So 0 is not an eigenvalue of $X^T X$. It follows that $X^T X$ is invertible. Then, we can solve the equation $X^T X\hat{\beta} = X^T y$ for $\hat{\beta}$ to get $\hat{\beta} =$

$(X^TX)^{-1}X^T\boldsymbol{y},$ which is the same result we got earlier using multi-variable calculus.

EXAMPLE: LINEAR REGRESSION

Suppose we have the following training data:

$(x_1, y_1) = (1, 1), (x_2, y_2) = (2, 4), (x_3, y_3) = (3, 4).$

Find the best fit line using the least squares method. Find the predicted value for $x = 4$.

Solution:

Form $X = \begin{bmatrix} 1 & 1 \\ 1 & 2 \\ 1 & 3 \end{bmatrix}$ and $\boldsymbol{y} = \begin{bmatrix} 1 \\ 4 \\ 4 \end{bmatrix}.$

The coefficients β_0, β_1 for the best fit line $f(x) = \beta_0 + \beta_1 x$ are given by $\begin{bmatrix} \beta_0 \\ \beta_1 \end{bmatrix} = (X^TX)^{-1}X^T\boldsymbol{y}.$

$X^T = \begin{bmatrix} 1 & 1 & 1 \\ 1 & 2 & 3 \end{bmatrix}$

$\Rightarrow \quad X^TX = \begin{bmatrix} 1 & 1 & 1 \\ 1 & 2 & 3 \end{bmatrix}\begin{bmatrix} 1 & 1 \\ 1 & 2 \\ 1 & 3 \end{bmatrix} = \begin{bmatrix} 3 & 6 \\ 6 & 14 \end{bmatrix}$

$\Rightarrow \quad (X^TX)^{-1} = \begin{bmatrix} 7/3 & -1 \\ -1 & 1/2 \end{bmatrix}$

$\Rightarrow \quad (X^TX)^{-1}X^T\boldsymbol{y} = \begin{bmatrix} 7/3 & -1 \\ -1 & 1/2 \end{bmatrix}\begin{bmatrix} 1 & 1 & 1 \\ 1 & 2 & 3 \end{bmatrix}\begin{bmatrix} 1 \\ 4 \\ 4 \end{bmatrix}$

$$= \begin{bmatrix} 0 \\ 3/2 \end{bmatrix}$$

$\Rightarrow \quad \beta_0 = 0$ and $\beta_1 = 3/2.$

Thus, the best fit line is given by $f(x) = \left(\frac{3}{2}\right)x.$

The predicted value for $x = 4$ is $f(4) = \left(\frac{3}{2}\right) \cdot 4 = 6.$

SUMMARY: LINEAR REGRESSION

- In the least squares method, we seek a linear function of the input variables that best fits the given training data. We do this by minimizing the residual sum of squares.

- To minimize the residual sum of squares, we apply the second derivative test from multi-variable calculus.

- We can arrive at the same solution to the least squares problem using linear algebra.

PROBLEM SET: LINEAR REGRESSION

1. Suppose we have the following training data:

   $(x_1, y_1) = (0, 2), (x_2, y_2) = (1, 1),$

   $(x_3, y_3) = (2, 4), (x_4, y_4) = (3, 4).$

   Find the best fit line using the least squares method. Find the predicted value for $x = 4$.

2. Suppose we have the following training data:

   $(x_1, y_1), (x_2, y_2), (x_3, y_3)$ where
   $$x_1 = \begin{bmatrix} 0 \\ 0 \end{bmatrix}, x_2 = \begin{bmatrix} 1 \\ 0 \end{bmatrix}, x_3 = \begin{bmatrix} 0 \\ 1 \end{bmatrix}, x_4 = \begin{bmatrix} 1 \\ 1 \end{bmatrix}$$
   and $y_1 = 1, y_2 = 0, y_3 = 0, y_4 = 2$.

   Find the best fit plane using the least squares method. Find the predicted value for $x = \begin{bmatrix} 2 \\ 2 \end{bmatrix}$.

SOLUTION SET: LINEAR REGRESSION

1. Form $X = \begin{bmatrix} 1 & 0 \\ 1 & 1 \\ 1 & 2 \\ 1 & 3 \end{bmatrix}$ and $y = \begin{bmatrix} 2 \\ 1 \\ 4 \\ 4 \end{bmatrix}$.

   The coefficients β_0, β_1 for the best fit line $f(x) = \beta_0 + \beta_1 x$ are given by $\begin{bmatrix} \beta_0 \\ \beta_1 \end{bmatrix} = (X^T X)^{-1} X^T y$.

$$X^T = \begin{bmatrix} 1 & 1 & 1 & 1 \\ 0 & 1 & 2 & 3 \end{bmatrix} \quad \Rightarrow \quad X^T X = \begin{bmatrix} 1 & 1 & 1 & 1 \\ 0 & 1 & 2 & 3 \end{bmatrix} \begin{bmatrix} 1 & 0 \\ 1 & 1 \\ 1 & 2 \\ 1 & 3 \end{bmatrix} = \begin{bmatrix} 4 & 6 \\ 6 & 14 \end{bmatrix}$$

$$\Rightarrow (X^T X)^{-1} = \begin{bmatrix} \frac{7}{10} & -\frac{3}{10} \\ -\frac{3}{10} & \frac{1}{5} \end{bmatrix}$$

$$\Rightarrow (X^T X)^{-1} X^T y = \begin{bmatrix} \frac{7}{10} & -\frac{3}{10} \\ -\frac{3}{10} & \frac{1}{5} \end{bmatrix} \begin{bmatrix} 1 & 1 & 1 & 1 \\ 0 & 1 & 2 & 3 \end{bmatrix} \begin{bmatrix} 2 \\ 1 \\ 4 \\ 4 \end{bmatrix}$$

$$= \begin{bmatrix} \frac{14}{10} \\ \frac{9}{10} \end{bmatrix}$$

$$\Rightarrow \beta_0 = \frac{14}{10} \quad \text{and} \quad \beta_1 = \frac{9}{10}.$$

   Thus, the best fit line is given by

$$f(x) = \frac{14}{10} + \frac{9}{10} x$$

   The predicted value for $x = 4$ is $f(4) = \frac{14}{10} + \frac{9}{10} \cdot 4 = 5$.

2. Form $X = \begin{bmatrix} 1 & 0 & 0 \\ 1 & 1 & 0 \\ 1 & 0 & 1 \\ 1 & 1 & 1 \end{bmatrix}$ and $y = \begin{bmatrix} 1 \\ 0 \\ 0 \\ 2 \end{bmatrix}$.

   The coefficients $\beta_0, \beta_1, \beta_2$ for the best fit line $f(x_1, x_2) = \beta_0 + \beta_1 x_1 + \beta_2 x_2$ are given by $\begin{bmatrix} \beta_0 \\ \beta_1 \\ \beta_2 \end{bmatrix} = (X^T X)^{-1} X^T y$.

$$X^T = \begin{bmatrix} 1 & 1 & 1 & 1 \\ 0 & 1 & 0 & 1 \\ 0 & 0 & 1 & 1 \end{bmatrix} \quad \Rightarrow \quad X^T X = \begin{bmatrix} 1 & 1 & 1 & 1 \\ 0 & 1 & 0 & 1 \\ 0 & 0 & 1 & 1 \end{bmatrix} \begin{bmatrix} 1 & 0 & 0 \\ 1 & 1 & 0 \\ 1 & 0 & 1 \\ 1 & 1 & 1 \end{bmatrix} = \begin{bmatrix} 4 & 2 & 2 \\ 2 & 2 & 1 \\ 2 & 1 & 2 \end{bmatrix}$$

$$\Rightarrow (X^T X)^{-1} = \begin{bmatrix} \frac{3}{4} & -\frac{1}{2} & -\frac{1}{2} \\ -\frac{1}{2} & 1 & 0 \\ -\frac{1}{2} & 0 & 1 \end{bmatrix}$$

$$\Rightarrow (X^T X)^{-1} X^T \boldsymbol{y} = \begin{bmatrix} \frac{3}{4} & -\frac{1}{2} & -\frac{1}{2} \\ -\frac{1}{2} & 1 & 0 \\ -\frac{1}{2} & 0 & 1 \end{bmatrix} \begin{bmatrix} 1 & 1 & 1 & 1 \\ 0 & 1 & 0 & 1 \\ 0 & 0 & 1 & 1 \end{bmatrix} \begin{bmatrix} 1 \\ 0 \\ 0 \\ 2 \end{bmatrix}$$

$$= \begin{bmatrix} \frac{3}{4} & \frac{1}{4} & \frac{1}{4} & -\frac{1}{4} \\ -\frac{1}{2} & \frac{1}{2} & -\frac{1}{2} & \frac{1}{2} \\ -\frac{1}{2} & -\frac{1}{2} & \frac{1}{2} & \frac{1}{2} \end{bmatrix} \begin{bmatrix} 1 \\ 0 \\ 0 \\ 2 \end{bmatrix}$$

$$= \begin{bmatrix} \frac{1}{4} \\ \frac{1}{2} \\ \frac{1}{2} \end{bmatrix}$$

$$\Rightarrow \beta_0 = \frac{1}{4} \quad , \quad \beta_1 = \frac{1}{2}, \beta_2 = \frac{1}{2}$$

Thus, the best fit plane is given by

$$f(x_1, x_2) = \frac{1}{4} + \frac{1}{2} x_1 + \frac{1}{2} x_2$$

The predicted value for $x = \begin{bmatrix} 2 \\ 2 \end{bmatrix}$ is $f(2, 2) = 2\frac{1}{4}$.

3 – LINEAR DISCRIMINANT ANALYSIS

CLASSIFICATION

In the problem of regression, we had a set of data $(x_1, y_1), \dots, (x_N, y_N)$ and we wanted to predict the values for the response variable Y for new data points. The values that Y took were numerical, quantitative, values. In certain problems, the values for the response variable Y that we want to predict are not quantitative but qualitative. So the values for Y will take on values from a finite set of classes or categories. Problems of this sort are called ***classification problems***. Some examples of a classification problem are classifying an email as spam or not spam and classifying a patient's illness as one among a finite number of diseases.

LINEAR DISCRIMINANT ANALYSIS

One method for solving a classification problem is called ***linear discriminant analysis***.

What we'll do is estimate $\Pr(Y = k | X = x)$, the probability that Y is the class k given that the input variable X is x. Once we have all of these probabilities for a fixed x, we pick the class k for which the probability $\Pr(Y = k | X = x)$ is largest. We then classify x as that class k.

THE POSTERIOR PROBABILITY FUNCTIONS

In this section, we'll build a formula for the posterior probability $\Pr(Y = k | X = x)$.

Let $\pi_k = \Pr(Y = k)$, the prior probability that $Y = k$.

Let $f_k(x) = \Pr(X = x | Y = k)$, the probability that $X = x$, given that $Y = k$.

By Bayes' rule,

$$\Pr(Y = k | X = x) = \frac{\Pr(X = x | Y = k) \cdot \Pr(Y = k)}{\sum_{l=1}^{K} \Pr(X = x | Y = l) \Pr(Y = l)}$$

Here we assume that k can take on the values $1, \dots, K$.

$$= \frac{f_k(x) \cdot \pi_k}{\sum_{l=1}^{K} f_l(x) \cdot \pi_l}$$

$$= \frac{\pi_k \cdot f_k(x)}{\sum_{l=1}^{K} \pi_l f_l(x)}$$

We can think of $\Pr(Y = k | X = x)$ as a function of x and denote it as $p_k(x)$.

So $p_k(x) = \frac{\pi_k \cdot f_k(x)}{\sum_{l=1}^{K} \pi_l f_l(x)}$. Recall that $p_k(x)$ is the posterior probability that $Y = k$ given that $X = x$.

MODELLING THE POSTERIOR PROBABILITY FUNCTIONS

Remember that we wanted to estimate $\Pr(Y = k | X = x)$ for any given x. That is, we want an estimate for $p_k(x)$. If we can get estimates for $\pi_k, f_k(x), \pi_l$ and $f_l(x)$ for each $l = 1, \dots, K$, then we would have an estimate for $p_k(x)$.

Let's say that $X = (X_1, X_2, \dots, X_p)$ where $X_1, \dots, X_p$ are the input variables. So the values of X will be vectors of p elements.

We will assume that the conditional distribution of X given $Y = k$ is the multivariate Gaussian distribution $N(\mu_k, \Sigma)$, where μ_k is a class-specific mean vector and Σ is the covariance of X.

The class-specific mean vector μ_k is given by the vector of class-specific means $\begin{bmatrix} \mu_{k1} \\ \vdots \\ \mu_{kp} \end{bmatrix}$, where μ_{kj} is the class-specific mean of X_j.

So $\mu_{kj} = \sum_{i: y_i = k} x_{ij} \Pr(X_j = x_{ij})$. Recall that $x_i = \begin{bmatrix} x_{i1} \\ \vdots \\ x_{ip} \end{bmatrix}$. (For all those x_i for which $y_i = k$, we're taking the mean of their jth components.)

Σ, the covariance matrix of X, is given by the matrix of covariances of X_i and X_j.

So $\Sigma = (a_{ij})$, where $a_{ij} = Cov(X_i, X_j) \stackrel{\text{def}}{=} E[(X_i - \mu_{X_i})(X_j - \mu_{X_j})]$.

The multivariate Gaussian density is given by
$$f(x) = \frac{1}{(2\pi)^{\frac{p}{2}} |\Sigma|^{\frac{1}{2}}} e^{-\frac{1}{2}(x-\mu)^T \Sigma^{-1}(x-\mu)}$$

for the multivariate Gaussian distribution $N(\mu, \Sigma)$.

Since we're assuming that the conditional distribution of X given $Y = k$ is the multivariate Gaussian distribution $N(\mu_k, \Sigma)$, we have that

$$\Pr(X = x | Y = k) = \frac{1}{(2\pi)^{\frac{p}{2}} |\Sigma|^{\frac{1}{2}}} e^{-\frac{1}{2}(x-\mu_k)^T \Sigma^{-1}(x-\mu_k)}.$$

Recall that $f_k(x) = \Pr(X = x | Y = k)$.
So $f_k(x) = \frac{1}{(2\pi)^{\frac{p}{2}} |\Sigma|^{\frac{1}{2}}} e^{-\frac{1}{2}(x-\mu_k)^T \Sigma^{-1}(x-\mu_k)}$.

Recall that $p_k(x) = \frac{\pi_k \cdot f_k(x)}{\sum_{l=1}^{K} \pi_l f_l(x)}$.

Plugging in what we have for $f_k(x)$, we get

$$p_k(x) = \frac{\pi_k \cdot \dfrac{1}{(2\pi)^{\frac{p}{2}}|\Sigma|^{\frac{1}{2}}}e^{-\frac{1}{2}(x-\mu_k)^T\Sigma^{-1}(x-\mu_k)}}{\sum_{l=1}^{K}\pi_l \cdot \dfrac{1}{(2\pi)^{\frac{p}{2}}|\Sigma|^{\frac{1}{2}}}e^{-\frac{1}{2}(x-\mu_l)^T\Sigma^{-1}(x-\mu_l)}}$$

$$= \frac{\pi_k \cdot e^{-\frac{1}{2}(x-\mu_k)^T\Sigma^{-1}(x-\mu_k)}}{\sum_{l=1}^{K}\pi_l \cdot e^{-\frac{1}{2}(x-\mu_l)^T\Sigma^{-1}(x-\mu_l)}} \, .$$

Note that the denominator is $(2\pi)^{\frac{p}{2}}|\Sigma|^{\frac{1}{2}}\sum_{l=1}^{K}\pi_l f_l(x)$ and that

$$\sum_{l=1}^{K}\pi_l f_l(x) = \sum_{l=1}^{K}f_l(x)\pi_l$$

$$= \sum_{l=1}^{K}\Pr(X=x|Y=l)\Pr(Y=l)$$

$$= \Pr(X=x).$$

So the denominator is just $(2\pi)^{\frac{p}{2}}|\Sigma|^{\frac{1}{2}}\Pr(X=x)$.

Hence, $p_k(x) = \dfrac{\pi_k \cdot e^{-\frac{1}{2}(x-\mu_k)^T\Sigma^{-1}(x-\mu_k)}}{(2\pi)^{\frac{p}{2}}|\Sigma|^{\frac{1}{2}}Pr(X=x)}.$

LINEAR DISCRIMINANT FUNCTIONS

Recall that we want to choose the class k for which the posterior probability $p_k(x)$ is largest. Since the logarithm function is order-preserving, maximizing $p_k(x)$ is the same as maximizing $\log p_k(x)$.

Taking $\log p_k(x)$ gives $\log \dfrac{\pi_k \cdot e^{-\frac{1}{2}(x-\mu_k)^T \Sigma^{-1}(x-\mu_k)}}{(2\pi)^{\frac{p}{2}}|\Sigma|^{\frac{1}{2}} Pr(X=x)}$

$$= \log \pi_k + \left(-\frac{1}{2}\right)(x-\mu_k)^T \Sigma^{-1}(x-\mu_k) - \log\left((2\pi)^{\frac{p}{2}}|\Sigma|^{\frac{1}{2}}\mathrm{Pr}(X=x)\right)$$

$$= log\, \pi_k + \left(-\frac{1}{2}\right)(x-\mu_k)^T \Sigma^{-1}(x-\mu_k) - \log C \qquad \text{where } C = (2\pi)^{\frac{p}{2}}|\Sigma|^{\frac{1}{2}}Pr(X=x).$$

$$= \log \pi_k - \frac{1}{2}(x^T \Sigma^{-1} - \mu_k^T \Sigma^{-1})(x-\mu_k) - \log C$$

$$= \log \pi_k - \frac{1}{2}[x^T \Sigma^{-1} x - x^T \Sigma^{-1}\mu_k - \mu_k^T \Sigma^{-1} x + \mu_k^T \Sigma^{-1}\mu_k] - \log C$$

$$= log\, \pi_k - \frac{1}{2}[x^T \Sigma^{-1} x - 2x^T \Sigma^{-1}\mu_k + \mu_k^T \Sigma^{-1}\mu_k] - log\, C,$$

$$\text{because } x^T \Sigma^{-1}\mu_k = \mu_k^T \Sigma^{-1} x$$
$$\text{Proof: } x^T \Sigma^{-1}\mu_k = \mu_k(\Sigma^{-1})^T x$$
$$= \mu_k^T (\Sigma^T)^{-1} x$$
$$= \mu_k^T \Sigma^{-1} x \text{ because } \Sigma \text{ is symmetric.}$$

$$= \log \pi_k - \frac{1}{2}x^T \Sigma^{-1} x + x^T \Sigma^{-1}\mu_k - \frac{1}{2}\mu_k^T \Sigma^{-1}\mu_k - \log C$$

$$= x^T \Sigma^{-1}\mu_k - \frac{1}{2}\mu_k^T \Sigma^{-1}\mu_k + \log \pi_k - \frac{1}{2}x^T \Sigma^{-1} x - \log C$$

Let $\delta_k(x) = x^T \Sigma^{-1}\mu_k - \frac{1}{2}\mu_k^T \Sigma^{-1}\mu_k + log\, \pi_k$.
Then $\log p_k(x) = \delta_k(x) - \frac{1}{2}x^T \Sigma^{-1} x - log\, C$.
$\delta_k(x)$ is called a **linear discriminant function**. Maximizing $\log p_k(x)$ is the same as maximizing $\delta_k(x)$ since $-\frac{1}{2}x^T \Sigma^{-1} x - \log C$ does not depend on k.

ESTIMATING THE LINEAR DISCRIMINANT FUNCTIONS

Now, if we can find estimates for π_k, μ_k, and Σ, then we would have an estimate for $p_k(x)$ and hence for $\log p_k(x)$ and $\delta_k(x)$.

In an attempt to maximize $p_k(x)$, we instead maximize the estimate of $p_k(x)$, which is the same as maximizing the estimate of $\delta_k(x)$.

π_k can be estimated as $\widehat{\pi_k} = \frac{N_k}{N}$ where N_k is the number of training data points in class k and N is the total number of training data points.

Remember $\pi_k = \Pr(Y = k)$. We're estimating this by just taking the proportion of data points in class k.

The class-specific mean vector $\mu_k = \begin{bmatrix} \mu_{k1} \\ \vdots \\ \mu_{kp} \end{bmatrix}$, where $\mu_{kj} = \sum_{i:y_i=k} x_{ij} \Pr(X_j = x_{ij})$.

We can estimate μ_{kj} as $\frac{1}{N_k}\sum_{i:y_i=k} x_{ij}$.

So we can estimate μ_k as $\widehat{\mu_k} = \begin{bmatrix} \frac{1}{N_k}\sum_{i:y_i=k} x_{i1} \\ \vdots \\ \frac{1}{N_k}\sum_{i:y_i=k} x_{ip} \end{bmatrix} = \frac{1}{N_k}\begin{bmatrix} \sum_{i:y_i=k} x_{i1} \\ \vdots \\ \sum_{i:y_i=k} x_{ip} \end{bmatrix}$

$$= \frac{1}{N_k}\sum_{i:y_i=k}\begin{bmatrix} x_{i1} \\ \vdots \\ x_{ip} \end{bmatrix}$$

$$= \frac{1}{N_k}\sum_{i:y_i=k} x_i$$

In other words, $\widehat{\mu_k} = \frac{1}{N_k}\sum_{i:y_i=k} x_i$. We estimate the class-specific mean vector by the vector of averages of each component over all x_i in class k.

Finally, the covariance matrix Σ is estimated as $\widehat{\Sigma} = \frac{1}{N-K}\sum_{k=1}^{K}\sum_{i:y_i=k}(x_i - \widehat{\mu_k})(x_i - \widehat{\mu_k})^T$.

Recall that $\delta_k(x) = x^T\Sigma^{-1}\mu_k - \frac{1}{2}\mu_k^T\Sigma^{-1}\mu_k + \log \pi_k$.

So, $\widehat{\delta_k}(x) = x^T\widehat{\Sigma}^{-1}\widehat{\mu_k} - \frac{1}{2}(\widehat{\mu_k})^T\widehat{\Sigma}^{-1}\widehat{\mu_k} + \log \widehat{\pi_k}$.

Note that $\widehat{\Sigma}, \widehat{\mu_k}$, and $\widehat{\pi_k}$ only depend on the training data and not on x. Note that x is a vector and $x^T\widehat{\Sigma}^{-1}\widehat{\mu_k}$ is a linear combination of the components of x. Hence, $\widehat{\delta_k}(x)$ is a linear combination of the components of x. This is why it's called a linear discriminant function.

CLASSIFYING DATA POINTS USING LINEAR DISCRIMINANT FUNCTIONS

If (k_1, k_2) is a pair of classes, we can consider whether $\widehat{\delta_{k_1}}(x) > \widehat{\delta_{k_2}}(x)$. If so, we know x is not in class k_2. Then, we can compare $\widehat{\delta_{k_1}}(x) > \widehat{\delta_{k_3}}(x)$ and rule out another class. Once we've exhausted all the classes, we'll know which class x should be assigned to.

Setting $\widehat{\delta_{k_1}}(x) = \widehat{\delta_{k_2}}(x)$, we get

$$x^T\widehat{\Sigma}^{-1}\widehat{\mu_{k_1}} - \frac{1}{2}\left(\widehat{\mu_{k_1}}\right)^T\widehat{\Sigma}^{-1}\widehat{\mu_{k_1}} + \log\widehat{\pi_{k_1}} = x^T\widehat{\Sigma}^{-1}\widehat{\mu_{k_2}} - \frac{1}{2}\left(\widehat{\mu_{k_2}}\right)^T\widehat{\Sigma}^{-1}\widehat{\mu_{k_2}} + \log\widehat{\pi_{k_2}}.$$

This gives us a hyperplane in $\mathbb{R}^p$ which separates class k_1 from class k_2.

If we find the separating hyperplane for each pair of classes, we get something like this:

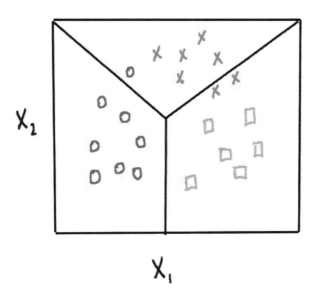

In this example, $p = 2$ and $K = 3$.

LDA EXAMPLE 1

Suppose we have a set of data $(x_1, y_1), \dots, (x_6, y_6)$ as follows:

$x_1 = (1,3), x_2 = (2,3), x_3 = (2,4), x_4 = (3,1), x_5 = (3,2), x_6 = (4,2),$

with $y_1 = y_2 = y_3 = k_1 = 1$ and $y_4 = y_5 = y_6 = k_2 = 2$.

Apply linear discriminant analysis by doing the following:

a) Find estimates for the linear discriminant functions $\delta_1(x)$ and $\delta_2(x)$.

b) Find the line that decides between the two classes.

c) Classify the new point $x = (5, 0)$.

Solution:

Here is a graph of the data points:

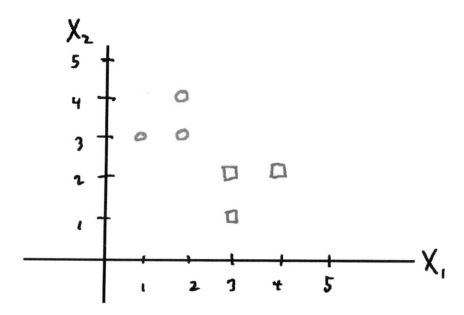

The number of features p is 2, the number of classes K is 2, the total number of data points N is 6, the number N_1 of data points in class k_1 is 3, and the number N_2 of data points in class k_2 is 3.

First, we will find estimates for π_1 and π_2, the prior probabilities that $Y = k_1$ and $Y = k_2$, respectively.

Then, we will find estimates for μ_1 and μ_2, the class-specific mean vectors.

We can then calculate the estimate for the covariance matrix Σ.

Finally, using the estimates $\widehat{\pi_1}, \widehat{\pi_2}, \widehat{\mu_1}, \widehat{\mu_2}, \widehat{\Sigma}$, we can find the estimates for the linear discriminant functions $\delta_1(x)$ and $\delta_2(x)$.

$$\widehat{\pi_1} = \frac{N_1}{N} = \frac{3}{6} = \frac{1}{2}$$

$$\widehat{\pi_2} = \frac{N_2}{N} = \frac{3}{6} = \frac{1}{2}$$

$$\widehat{\mu_1} = \frac{1}{N_1} \sum_{i:y_i=1} x_i = \frac{1}{3}[x_1 + x_2 + x_3] = \begin{bmatrix} 5/3 \\ 10/3 \end{bmatrix}$$

$$\widehat{\mu_2} = \frac{1}{N_2} \sum_{i:y_i=2} x_i = \frac{1}{3}[x_4 + x_5 + x_6] = \begin{bmatrix} 10/3 \\ 5/3 \end{bmatrix}$$

$$\widehat{\Sigma} = \frac{1}{N-K} \sum_{k=1}^{K} \sum_{i:y_i=k} (x_i - \widehat{\mu_k})(x_i - \widehat{\mu_k})^T$$

$$= \frac{1}{6-2} \sum_{k=1}^{2} \sum_{i:y_i=k} (x_i - \widehat{\mu_k})(x_i - \widehat{\mu_k})^T$$

Plugging in what we got for $\widehat{\mu_1}$ and $\widehat{\mu_2}$, we get

$$\widehat{\Sigma} = \frac{1}{4} \begin{bmatrix} 4/3 & 2/3 \\ 2/3 & 4/3 \end{bmatrix} = \begin{bmatrix} 1/3 & 1/6 \\ 1/6 & 1/3 \end{bmatrix}$$

$$\Rightarrow \widehat{\Sigma}^{-1} = \begin{bmatrix} 4 & -2 \\ -2 & 4 \end{bmatrix}$$

$$\widehat{\delta_1}(x) = x^T \widehat{\Sigma}^{-1} \widehat{\mu_1} - \frac{1}{2}(\widehat{\mu_1})^T \widehat{\Sigma}^{-1} \widehat{\mu_1} + \log \widehat{\pi_1}.$$

$$= x^T \begin{bmatrix} 0 \\ 10 \end{bmatrix} - \frac{1}{2}\left(\frac{100}{3}\right) + \log \frac{1}{2}$$

$$= 10X_2 - \frac{50}{3} + \log \frac{1}{2}$$

$$\widehat{\delta_2}(x) = x^T \widehat{\Sigma}^{-1} \widehat{\mu_2} - \frac{1}{2}(\widehat{\mu_2})^T \widehat{\Sigma}^{-1} \widehat{\mu_2} + \log \widehat{\pi_2}.$$

$$= x^T \begin{bmatrix} 10 \\ 0 \end{bmatrix} - \frac{1}{2}\left(\frac{100}{3}\right) + \log \frac{1}{2}$$

$$= 10X_1 - \frac{50}{3} + \log \frac{1}{2}$$

Setting $\widehat{\delta_1}(x) = \widehat{\delta_2}(x)$

$$\Rightarrow \qquad 10X_2 - \frac{50}{3} + \log \frac{1}{2} = 10X_1 - \frac{50}{3} + \log \frac{1}{2}$$

$$\Rightarrow \qquad 10X_2 = 10X_1$$

$$\Rightarrow \qquad X_2 = X_1.$$

So, the line that decides between the two classes is given by $X_2 = X_1$.

Here is a graph of the deciding line:

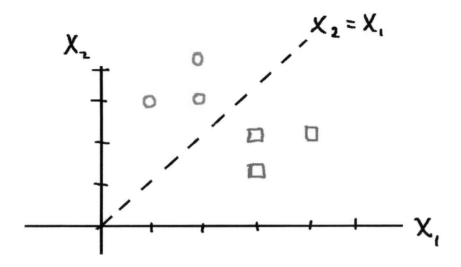

If $\widehat{\delta_1}(x) > \widehat{\delta_2}(x)$, then we classify x as of class k_1. So if x is above the line $X_2 = X_1$, then we classify x as of class k_1. Conversely, if $\widehat{\delta_1}(x) < \widehat{\delta_2}(x)$, then we classify x as of class k_2. This corresponds to x being below the line $X_2 = X_1$.

The point $(5, 0)$ is below the line; so we classify it as of class k_2.

LDA EXAMPLE 2

Suppose we have a set of data $(x_1, y_1), \ldots, (x_6, y_6)$ as follows:

$x_1 = (0, 2), x_2 = (1, 2), x_3 = (2, 0), x_4 = (2, 1), x_5 = (3, 3), x_6 = (4, 4),$

with $y_1 = y_2 = k_1 = 1$, $y_3 = y_4 = k_2 = 2$, and $y_5 = y_6 = k_3 = 3$.

Apply linear discriminant analysis by doing the following:

a) Find estimates for the linear discriminant functions $\delta_1(x), \delta_2(x)$, and $\delta_3(x)$.
b) Find the lines that decide between each pair of classes.
c) Classify the new point $x = (1, 3)$.

Solution:

Here is a graph of the data points:

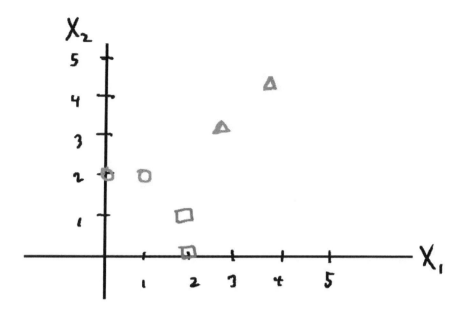

The number of features p is 2, the number of classes K is 3, the total number of data points N is 6, the number N_1 of data points in class k_1 is 2, the number N_2 of data points in class k_2 is 2, and the number N_3 of data points in class k_3 is 2.

First, we will find estimates for π_1, π_2, π_3, the prior probabilities that $Y = k_1$, $Y = k_2$, $Y = k_3$, respectively.

Then, we will find estimates for μ_1, μ_2, μ_3, the class-specific mean vectors.

We can then calculate the estimate for the covariance matrix Σ.

Finally, using the estimates $\widehat{\pi_1}, \widehat{\pi_2}, \widehat{\pi_3}, \widehat{\mu_1}, \widehat{\mu_2}, \widehat{\mu_3}, \widehat{\Sigma}$, we can find the estimates for the linear discriminant functions $\delta_1(x), \delta_2(x)$, and $\delta_3(x)$.

$$\widehat{\pi_1} = \frac{N_1}{N} = \frac{2}{6} = \frac{1}{3}$$

$$\widehat{\pi_2} = \frac{N_2}{N} = \frac{2}{6} = \frac{1}{3}$$

$$\widehat{\pi_3} = \frac{N_3}{N} = \frac{2}{6} = \frac{1}{3}$$

$$\widehat{\mu_1} = \frac{1}{N_1} \sum_{i:y_i=1} x_i = \frac{1}{2}[x_1 + x_2] = \begin{bmatrix} 1/2 \\ 2 \end{bmatrix}$$

$$\widehat{\mu_2} = \frac{1}{N_2} \sum_{i:y_i=2} x_i = \frac{1}{2}[x_3 + x_4] = \begin{bmatrix} 2 \\ 1/2 \end{bmatrix}$$

$$\widehat{\mu_3} = \frac{1}{N_3} \sum_{i:y_i=3} x_i = \frac{1}{2}[x_5 + x_6] = \begin{bmatrix} 7/2 \\ 7/2 \end{bmatrix}$$

$$\widehat{\Sigma} = \frac{1}{N-K} \sum_{k=1}^{K} \sum_{i:y_i=k} (x_i - \widehat{\mu_k})(x_i - \widehat{\mu_k})^T$$

$$= \frac{1}{6-3} \begin{bmatrix} 1 & 1/2 \\ 1/2 & 1 \end{bmatrix} = \begin{bmatrix} 1/3 & 1/6 \\ 1/6 & 1/3 \end{bmatrix}$$

$$\Rightarrow \quad \widehat{\Sigma}^{-1} = \begin{bmatrix} 4 & -2 \\ -2 & 4 \end{bmatrix}$$

$$\widehat{\delta_1}(x) = x^T \widehat{\Sigma}^{-1} \widehat{\mu_1} - \frac{1}{2}(\widehat{\mu_1})^T \widehat{\Sigma}^{-1} \widehat{\mu_1} + \log \widehat{\pi_1}.$$

$$= x^T \begin{bmatrix} -2 \\ 7 \end{bmatrix} - \left(\frac{13}{2}\right) + \log \frac{1}{3}$$

$$= -2X_1 + 7X_2 - \frac{13}{2} + \log \frac{1}{3}$$

$$\widehat{\delta_2}(x) = x^T \widehat{\Sigma}^{-1} \widehat{\mu_2} - \frac{1}{2}(\widehat{\mu_2})^T \widehat{\Sigma}^{-1} \widehat{\mu_2} + \log \widehat{\pi_2}.$$

$$= x^T \begin{bmatrix} 7 \\ -2 \end{bmatrix} - \left(\frac{13}{2}\right) + \log \frac{1}{3}$$

$$= 7X_1 - 2X_2 - \frac{13}{2} + \log \frac{1}{3}$$

$$\widehat{\delta_3}(x) = x^T \widehat{\Sigma}^{-1} \widehat{\mu_3} - \frac{1}{2}(\widehat{\mu_3})^T \widehat{\Sigma}^{-1} \widehat{\mu_3} + \log \widehat{\pi_3}.$$

$$= x^T \begin{bmatrix} 7 \\ 7 \end{bmatrix} - \left(\frac{49}{2}\right) + \log \frac{1}{3}$$

$$= 7X_1 + 7X_2 - \frac{49}{2} + \log \frac{1}{3}$$

Setting $\widehat{\delta_1}(x) = \widehat{\delta_2}(x)$

$$\Rightarrow \quad -2X_1 + 7X_2 - \frac{13}{2} + \log\frac{1}{3} = 7X_1 - 2X_2 - \frac{13}{2} + \log\frac{1}{3}$$

$$\Rightarrow \quad -2X_1 + 7X_2 = 7X_1 - 2X_2$$

$$\Rightarrow \quad 9X_2 = 9X_1$$

$$\Rightarrow \qquad X_2 = X_1.$$

So, the line that decides between classes k_1 and k_2 is given by $X_2 = X_1$.

Setting $\widehat{\delta_1}(x) = \widehat{\delta_3}(x)$
$$\Rightarrow \qquad -2X_1 + 7X_2 - \frac{13}{2} + log\frac{1}{3} = 7X_1 + 7X_2 - \frac{49}{2} + log\frac{1}{3}$$

$$\Rightarrow \qquad 18 = 9X_1$$

$$\Rightarrow \qquad X_1 = 2$$

So, the line that decides between classes k_1 and k_3 is given by $X_1 = 2$.

Setting $\widehat{\delta_2}(x) = \widehat{\delta_3}(x)$
$$\Rightarrow \qquad 7X_1 - 2X_2 - \frac{13}{2} + log\frac{1}{3} = 7X_1 + 7X_2 - \frac{49}{2} + log\frac{1}{3}$$

$$\Rightarrow \qquad 18 = 9X_2$$

$$\Rightarrow \qquad X_2 = 2$$

So, the line that decides between classes k_2 and k_3 is given by $X_2 = 2$.

Here is a graph of the deciding lines:

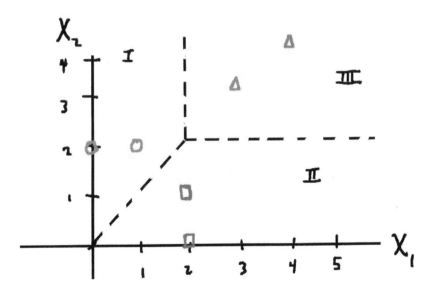

The lines divide the plane into 3 regions.

$\widehat{\delta_1}(x) > \widehat{\delta_2}(x)$ corresponds to the region above the line $X_2 = X_1$. Conversely, $\widehat{\delta_1}(x) < \widehat{\delta_2}(x)$ corresponds to the region below the line $X_2 = X_1$.

$\widehat{\delta_1}(x) > \widehat{\delta_3}(x)$ corresponds to the region to the left of the line $X_1 = 2$. Conversely, $\widehat{\delta_1}(x) < \widehat{\delta_3}(x)$

corresponds to the region to the right of $X_1 = 2$.

$\widehat{\delta_2}(x) > \widehat{\delta_3}(x)$ corresponds to the region below the line $X_2 = 2$. Conversely, $\widehat{\delta_2}(x) < \widehat{\delta_3}(x)$ corresponds to the region above the line $X_2 = 2$.

If $\widehat{\delta_1}(x) > \widehat{\delta_2}(x)$ and $\widehat{\delta_1}(x) > \widehat{\delta_3}(x)$, then we classify x as of class k_1. So if x is in region I, then we classify x as of class k_1. Conversely, if x is in region II, then we classify x as of class k_2; and if x is in region III, we classify x as of class k_3.

The point $(1, 3)$ is in region I; so we classify it as of class k_1.

SUMMARY: LINEAR DISCRIMINANT ANALYSIS

- In linear discriminant analysis, we find estimates $\widehat{p_k}(x)$ for the posterior probability $p_k(x)$ that $Y = k$ given that $X = x$. We classify x according to the class k that gives the highest estimated posterior probability $\widehat{p_k}(x)$.

- Maximizing the estimated posterior probability $\widehat{p_k}(x)$ is equivalent to maximizing the log of $\widehat{p_k}(x)$, which, in turn, is equivalent to maximizing the estimated linear discriminant function $\widehat{\delta_k}(x)$.

- We find estimates of the prior probability π_k that $Y = k$, of the class-specific mean vectors μ_k, and of the covariance matrix Σ in order to estimate the linear discriminant functions $\delta_k(x)$.

- By setting $\widehat{\delta_k}(x) = \widehat{\delta_{k'}}(x)$ for each pair (k, k') of classes, we get hyperplanes in $\mathbb{R}^p$ that, together, divide $\mathbb{R}^p$ into regions corresponding to the distinct classes.

- We classify x according to the class k for which $\widehat{\delta_k}(x)$ is largest.

PROBLEM SET: LINEAR DISCRIMINANT ANALYSIS

1. Suppose we have a set of data $(x_1, y_1), \dots, (x_6, y_6)$ as follows:

   $x_1 = (1, 2), x_2 = (2, 1), x_3 = (2, 2), x_4 = (3, 3), x_5 = (3, 4), x_6 = (4, 3)$ with

   $y_1 = y_2 = y_3 = k_1 = 1$ and $y_4 = y_5 = y_6 = k_2 = 2$.

   Apply linear discriminant analysis by doing the following:

   a) Find estimates for the linear discriminant functions $\delta_1(x)$ and $\delta_2(x)$.

   b) Find the line that decides between the two classes.

   c) Classify the new point $x = (4, 5)$.

2. Suppose we have a set of data $(x_1, y_1), \dots, (x_6, y_6)$ as follows:

   $x_1 = (0, 0), x_2 = (1, 1), x_3 = (2, 3), x_4 = (2, 4), x_5 = (3, 2), x_6 = (4, 2)$ with

   $y_1 = y_2 = k_1 = 1, y_3 = y_4 = k_2 = 2$ and $y_5 = y_6 = k_3 = 3$.

   Apply linear discriminant analysis by doing the following:

   a) Find estimates for the linear discriminant functions $\delta_1(x)$, $\delta_2(x)$ and $\delta_3(x)$.

   b) Find the lines that decide between each pair of classes.

   c) Classify the new point $x = (3, 0)$.

SOLUTION SET: LINEAR DISCRIMINANT ANALYSIS

1. Here is a graph of the data points:

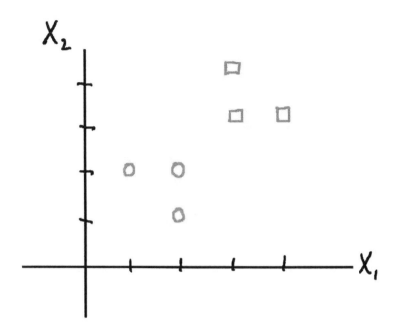

The number of features p is 2, the number of classes K is 2, the total number of data points N is 6, the number N_1 of data points in class k_1 is 3, and the number N_2 of data points in class k_2 is 3.

First, we will find estimates for π_1 and π_2, the prior probabilities that $Y = k_1$ and $Y = k_2$, respectively.

Then, we will find estimates for μ_1 and μ_2, the class-specific mean vectors.

We can then calculate the estimate for the covariance matrix Σ.

Finally, using the estimates $\widehat{\pi_1}, \widehat{\pi_2}, \widehat{\mu_1}, \widehat{\mu_2}, \widehat{\Sigma}$, we can find the estimates for the linear discriminant functions $\delta_1(x)$ and $\delta_2(x)$.

$$\widehat{\pi_1} = \frac{N_1}{N} = \frac{3}{6} = \frac{1}{2}$$

$$\widehat{\pi_2} = \frac{N_2}{N} = \frac{3}{6} = \frac{1}{2}$$

$$\widehat{\mu_1} = \frac{1}{N_1} \sum_{i:y_i=1} x_i = \frac{1}{3}[x_1 + x_2 + x_3] = \begin{bmatrix} \frac{5}{3} \\ \frac{5}{3} \end{bmatrix}$$

$$\widehat{\mu_2} = \frac{1}{N_2} \sum_{i:y_i=2} x_i = \frac{1}{3}[x_4 + x_5 + x_6] = \begin{bmatrix} \frac{10}{3} \\ \frac{10}{3} \end{bmatrix}$$

$$\widehat{\Sigma} = \frac{1}{N-K} \sum_{k=1}^{K} \sum_{i:y_i=k} (x_i - \widehat{\mu_k})(x_i - \widehat{\mu_k})^T$$

$$= \frac{1}{6-2} \begin{bmatrix} 12/9 & -6/9 \\ -6/9 & 12/9 \end{bmatrix} = \begin{bmatrix} 1/3 & -1/6 \\ -1/6 & 1/3 \end{bmatrix}$$

$$\Rightarrow \quad \widehat{\Sigma}^{-1} = \begin{bmatrix} 4 & 2 \\ 2 & 4 \end{bmatrix}$$

$$\widehat{\delta_1}(x) = x^T \widehat{\Sigma}^{-1} \widehat{\mu_1} - \frac{1}{2} \widehat{\mu_1}^T \widehat{\Sigma}^{-1} \widehat{\mu_1} + \log \widehat{\pi_1}$$

$$= x^T \begin{bmatrix} 10 \\ 10 \end{bmatrix} - \frac{1}{2}\left(\frac{100}{3}\right) + \log \frac{1}{2}$$

$$= 10X_1 + 10X_2 - \frac{50}{3} + \log \frac{1}{2}$$

$$\widehat{\delta_2}(x) = x^T \widehat{\Sigma}^{-1} \widehat{\mu_2} - \frac{1}{2} \widehat{\mu_2}^T \widehat{\Sigma}^{-1} \widehat{\mu_2} + \log \widehat{\pi_2}$$

$$= x^T \begin{bmatrix} 20 \\ 20 \end{bmatrix} - \frac{1}{2}\left(\frac{400}{3}\right) + \log \frac{1}{2}$$

$$= 20X_1 + 20X_2 - \frac{200}{3} + \log \frac{1}{2}$$

Setting $\widehat{\delta_1}(x) = \widehat{\delta_2}(x)$

$$\Rightarrow \quad 10X_1 + 10X_2 - \frac{50}{3} + \log \frac{1}{2} = 20X_1 + 20X_2 - \frac{200}{3} + \log \frac{1}{2}$$

$$\Rightarrow \quad \frac{150}{3} = 10X_1 + 10X_2$$

$$\Rightarrow \quad 50 = 10X_1 + 10X_2$$

$$\Rightarrow \quad 5 = X_1 + X_2$$

$$\Rightarrow \quad -X_1 + 5 = X_2$$

So, the line that decides between the two classes is given by $X_2 = -X_1 + 5$.

Here is a graph of the decision line:

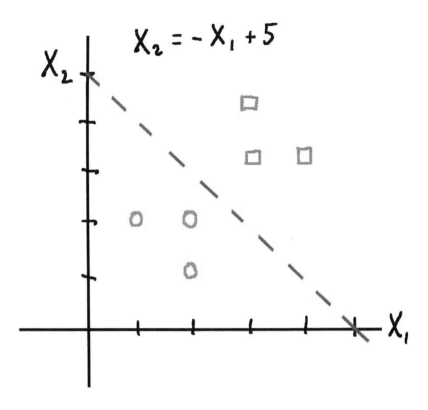

If $\widehat{\delta_1}(x) > \widehat{\delta_2}(x)$, then we classify x as of class k_1.

So if x is below the line $X_2 = -X_1 + 5$, then we classify x as of class k_1.

Conversely, if $\widehat{\delta_1}(x) < \widehat{\delta_2}(x)$, then we classify x as of class k_2. This corresponds to x being above the line $X_2 = -X_1 + 5$.

The point $(4, 5)$ is above the line; so we classify it as of class k_2.

2. Here is a graph of the data points:

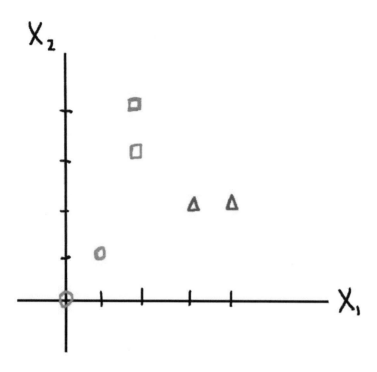

The number of features p is 2, the number of classes K is 3, the total number of data points N is 6, the number N_1 of data points in class k_1 is 2, the number N_2 of data points in class k_2 is 2, and the number N_3 of data points in class k_3 is 2.

First, we will find estimates for π_1, π_2, π_3, the prior probabilities that $Y = k_1, Y = k_2, Y = k_3$, respectively.

Then, we will find estimates for μ_1, μ_2, μ_3, the class-specific mean vectors.

We can then calculate the estimate for the covariance matrix Σ.

Finally, using the estimates $\widehat{\pi_1}, \widehat{\pi_2}, \widehat{\pi_3}, \widehat{\mu_1}, \widehat{\mu_2}, \widehat{\mu_3}, \widehat{\Sigma}$, we can find the estimates for the linear discriminant functions $\delta_1(x)$, $\delta_2(x)$, and $\delta_3(x)$.

$$\widehat{\pi_1} = \frac{N_1}{N} = \frac{2}{6} = \frac{1}{3}$$
$$\widehat{\pi_2} = \frac{N_2}{N} = \frac{2}{6} = \frac{1}{3}$$
$$\widehat{\pi_3} = \frac{N_3}{N} = \frac{2}{6} = \frac{1}{3}$$

$$\widehat{\mu_1} = \frac{1}{N_1} \sum_{i:y_i=1} x_i = \frac{1}{2}[x_1 + x_2] = \begin{bmatrix} 1/2 \\ 1/2 \end{bmatrix}$$

$$\widehat{\mu_2} = \frac{1}{N_2} \sum_{i:y_i=2} x_i = \frac{1}{2}[x_3 + x_4] = \begin{bmatrix} 2 \\ 7/2 \end{bmatrix}$$

$$\widehat{\mu_3} = \frac{1}{N_3} \sum_{i:y_i=3} x_i = \frac{1}{2}[x_5 + x_6] = \begin{bmatrix} 7/2 \\ 2 \end{bmatrix}$$

$$\widehat{\Sigma} = \frac{1}{N-K} \sum_{k=1}^{K} \sum_{i:y_i=k} (x_i - \widehat{\mu_k})(x_i - \widehat{\mu_k})^T$$

$$= \frac{1}{6-3} \begin{bmatrix} 1 & 1/2 \\ 1/2 & 1 \end{bmatrix} = \begin{bmatrix} 1/3 & 1/6 \\ 1/6 & 1/3 \end{bmatrix}$$

$$\implies \widehat{\Sigma}^{-1} = \begin{bmatrix} 4 & -2 \\ -2 & 4 \end{bmatrix}$$

$$\widehat{\delta_1}(x) = x^T \widehat{\Sigma}^{-1} \widehat{\mu_1} - \frac{1}{2} \widehat{\mu_1}^T \widehat{\Sigma}^{-1} \widehat{\mu_1} + \log \widehat{\pi_1}$$

$$= x^T \begin{bmatrix} 1 \\ 1 \end{bmatrix} - \frac{1}{2}(1) + \log \frac{1}{3}$$

$$= X_1 + X_2 - \frac{1}{2} + \log \frac{1}{3}$$

$$\widehat{\delta_2}(x) = x^T \widehat{\Sigma}^{-1} \widehat{\mu_2} - \frac{1}{2} \widehat{\mu_2}^T \widehat{\Sigma}^{-1} \widehat{\mu_2} + \log \widehat{\pi_2}$$

$$= x^T \begin{bmatrix} 1 \\ 10 \end{bmatrix} - \frac{1}{2}(37) + \log \frac{1}{3}$$

$$= X_1 + 10X_2 - \frac{37}{2} + \log \frac{1}{3}$$

$$\widehat{\delta_3}(x) = x^T \widehat{\Sigma}^{-1} \widehat{\mu_3} - \frac{1}{2} \widehat{\mu_3}^T \widehat{\Sigma}^{-1} \widehat{\mu_3} + \log \widehat{\pi_3}$$

$$= x^T \begin{bmatrix} 10 \\ 1 \end{bmatrix} - \frac{1}{2}(37) + \log \frac{1}{3}$$

$$= 10X_1 + X_2 - \frac{37}{2} + \log \frac{1}{3}$$

Setting $\widehat{\delta_1}(x) = \widehat{\delta_2}(x)$

$$\implies X_1 + X_2 - \frac{1}{2} + \log \frac{1}{3} = X_1 + 10X_2 - \frac{37}{2} + \log \frac{1}{3}$$

$$\implies 18 = 9X_2$$

$$\implies 2 = X_2$$

So, the line that decides between classes k_1 and k_2 is given by $X_2 = 2$.

Setting $\widehat{\delta_1}(x) = \widehat{\delta_3}(x)$

$\Longrightarrow \quad X_1 + X_2 - \frac{1}{2} + \log\frac{1}{3} = 10X_1 + X_2 - \frac{37}{2} + \log\frac{1}{3}$

$\Longrightarrow \quad 18 = 9X_1$

$\Longrightarrow \quad 2 = X_1$

So, the line that decides between classes k_1 and k_3 is given by $X_1 = 2$.

Setting $\widehat{\delta_2}(x) = \widehat{\delta_3}(x)$

$\Longrightarrow X_1 + 10X_2 - \frac{37}{2} + \log\frac{1}{3} = 10X_1 + X_2 - \frac{37}{2} + \log\frac{1}{3}$

$\Longrightarrow 9X_2 = 9X_1$

$\Longrightarrow X_2 = X_1$

So, the line that decides between classes k_2 and k_3 is given by $X_2 = X_1$.

Here is a graph of the decision lines:

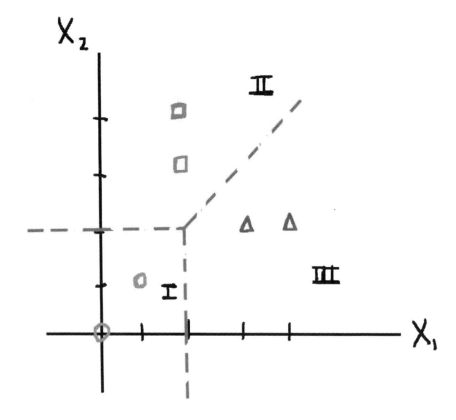

The lines divide the plane into 3 regions.

If x is in region I, then we classify x as of class k_1. Similarly, points in region II get classified as of k_2, and points in region III get classified as of k_3.

The point $(3, 0)$ is in region III; so we classify it as of class k_3.

4 – LOGISTIC REGRESSION

LOGISTIC REGRESSION

In this section, we'll look at another method for classification problems called ***logistic regression***.

Just as in linear discriminant analysis, we want to estimate $\Pr(Y = k | X = x)$ and pick the class k for which this probability is largest. Instead of estimating this probability indirectly using Bayes' rule, as in linear discriminant analysis, we'll estimate the probability directly.

Since logistic regression is more commonly used in the case of $K = 2$ classes, we will focus on that case in this section. We will denote the two classes by 0 and 1. An example in which logistic regression with 2 classes can be applied is in determining whether a patient has a certain form of cancer or not.

LOGISTIC REGRESSION MODEL OF THE POSTERIOR PROBABILITY FUNCTION

Let $p(x) = \Pr(Y = 1 | X = x)$.

Consider $\frac{p(x)}{1-p(x)}$. This is called the ***odds***.

Now take $\log \frac{p(x)}{1-p(x)}$. This is called the ***log-odds***.

In logistic regression, we assume that the log-odds is a linear function of the components of x.

In other words, $\log \frac{p(x)}{1-p(x)} = \beta_0 + \beta_1 x_1 + \cdots + \beta_p x_p$ where $x = \begin{bmatrix} x_1 \\ \vdots \\ x_p \end{bmatrix}$.

Solving for $p(x)$, we get:

$$\frac{p(x)}{1 - p(x)} = e^{\beta_0 + \beta_1 x_1 + \cdots + \beta_p x_p}$$

$$\implies p(x) = e^{\beta_0 + \beta_1 x_1 + \cdots + \beta_p x_p} - e^{\beta_0 + \beta_1 x_1 + \cdots + \beta_p x_p} \cdot p(x)$$

$$\implies p(x) = \frac{e^{\beta_0 + \beta_1 x_1 + \cdots + \beta_p x_p}}{1 + e^{\beta_0 + \beta_1 x_1 + \cdots + \beta_p x_p}}$$

This is the probability $\Pr(Y = 1 | X = x)$ that we want to estimate. To do this, we need estimates for the parameters $\beta_0, \ldots, \beta_p$.

ESTIMATING THE POSTERIOR PROBABILITY FUNCTION

Let's say our training data is $(z_1, y_1), \ldots, (z_N, y_N)$. The y values are either 0 or 1. The probability of the observed data is given by the product of the probabilities that $Y = 1$ for those z_i whose y value is 1 and the probabilities that $Y = 0$ for those z_i whose y value is 0. That is,

$$\prod_{i:y_i=1} \Pr(Y = 1 | X = z_i) \prod_{i:y_i=0} \Pr(Y = 0 | X = z_i)$$

Since $\Pr(Y = 0 | X = z_i) = 1 - \Pr(Y = 1 | X = z_i)$, we can rewrite the product as

$$\prod_{i:y_i=1} \Pr(Y = 1 | X = z_i) \prod_{i:y_i=0} (1 - \Pr(Y = 1 | X = z_i))$$

$$= \prod_{i:y_i=1} p(z_i) \prod_{i:y_i=0} (1 - p(z_i))$$

We want to find estimates for $\beta_0, \ldots, \beta_p$ that maximize the probability of our observed data given by $\prod_{i:y_i=1} p(z_i) \prod_{i:y_i=0} (1 - p(z_i))$.

Let $l(\beta_0, \ldots, \beta_p) = \prod_{i:y_i=1} p(z_i) \prod_{i:y_i=0} (1 - p(z_i))$. This is called a **likelihood function**.

Thus, to find estimates for $\beta_0, \ldots, \beta_p$, we want to maximize the likelihood function.

Letting $\beta = (\beta_0, \beta_1, \ldots, \beta_p)$, we can rewrite the likelihood function as

$l(\beta) = \prod_{i:y_i=1} p(z_i) \prod_{i:y_i=0} (1 - p(z_i))$.

Recall that $(x) = \frac{e^{\beta_0+\beta_1 x_1+\cdots+\beta_p x_p}}{1+e^{\beta_0+\beta_1 x_1+\cdots+\beta_p x_p}}$. So $p(x)$ depends on the parameters $\beta_0, \beta_1, \ldots, \beta_p$. To indicate this dependence, we'll write $p(x; \beta)$ for $p(x)$.

So $l(\beta) = \prod_{i:y_i=1} p(z_i; \beta) \prod_{i:y_i=0} (1 - p(z_i; \beta))$.

Maximizing the likelihood function is the same as maximizing the log of the likelihood function.

So let $L(\beta) = \log l(\beta) = \log \prod_{i:y_i=1} p(z_i; \beta) \prod_{i:y_i=0} (1 - p(z_i; \beta))$. This is called the **log-likelihood function**.

We'll try to maximize $L(\beta)$.

Note that $L(\beta) = \sum_{i:y_i=1} \log p(z_i; \beta) + \sum_{i:y_i=0} \log(1 - p(z_i; \beta))$

$$= \sum_{i=1}^{N} [y_i \log p(z_i; \beta) + (1 - y_i) \log(1 - p(z_i; \beta))]$$

$$= \sum_{i=1}^{N} [y_i[\log p(z_i; \beta) - \log(1 - p(z_i; \beta))] + \log(1 - p(z_i; \beta))]$$

$$= \sum_{i=1}^{N} \left[y_i \log \left(\frac{p(z_i; \beta)}{1 - p(z_i; \beta)} \right) + \log(1 - p(z_i; \beta)) \right]$$

$$= \sum_{i=1}^{N} \left[y_i \log e^{\beta^T z_i'} + \log \frac{1}{1 + e^{\beta^T z_i'}} \right],$$

where $z_i' = \begin{bmatrix} 1 \\ z_{i1} \\ \vdots \\ z_{ip} \end{bmatrix}$. To see this, note that

$$p(z_i; \beta) = \frac{e^{\beta^T z_i'}}{1 + e^{\beta^T z_i'}} \text{ where } z_i' = \begin{bmatrix} 1 \\ z_{i1} \\ \vdots \\ z_{ip} \end{bmatrix}. \text{ So } 1 -$$

$$p(z_i; \beta) = \frac{1}{1 + e^{\beta^T z_i'}} \text{ and } \frac{p(z_i; \beta)}{1 - p(z_i; \beta)} = e^{\beta^T z_i'}.$$

$$= \sum_{i=1}^{N} [y_i \beta^T z_i' - \log(1 + e^{\beta^T z_i'})]$$

So $L(\beta) = \sum_{i=1}^{N} [y_i \beta^T z_i' - \log(1 + e^{\beta^T z_i'})]$.

To maximize $L(\beta)$, we will use the multivariate Newton-Raphson method. Let's look at how the method works, and we'll return to $L(\beta)$.

THE MULTIVARIATE NEWTON-RAPIISON METHOD

Suppose $f: \mathbb{R}^k \longrightarrow \mathbb{R}$ is twice continuously differentiable. Suppose $x \in \mathbb{R}^k$ is near $a \in \mathbb{R}^k$. Then, the second order Taylor approximation of $f(x)$ gives

$$f(x) \approx f(a) + \left(\nabla f(a)\right)^T (x - a) + \frac{1}{2}(x - a)^T H(x - a),$$

where $\nabla f(a)$ is the gradient of f evaluated at a and H is the Hessian of f evaluated at a.

Now, let's say we want to maximize f. The Newton-Raphson method says to first pick an initial x-value a. Then, consider the second order Taylor approximation of $f(x)$ for x near a:

$$f(x) \approx f(a) + \left(\nabla f(a)\right)^T (x - a) + \frac{1}{2}(x - a)^T H(x - a)$$

Find the maximum of the second order approximation by taking the gradient of the second order approximation and setting it to 0.

Letting $q(x) = f(a) + \left(\nabla f(a)\right)^T (x - a) + \frac{1}{2}(x - a)^T H(x - a)$, we want to find $\nabla q(x)$ and set it to 0.

$$\nabla q(x) = \nabla\big(f(a)\big) + \nabla\left[\left(\nabla f(a)\right)^T (x - a)\right] + \frac{1}{2}\nabla[(x - a)^T H(x - a)]$$

$$= \mathbf{0} + \nabla f(a) + \frac{1}{2}\nabla[(x - a)^T H(x - a)],$$

> because $\nabla(b^T x) = b$ combined with the multivariable chain rule. (The Jacobian of $g(x) = x - a$ is I.)

$$= \nabla f(a) + \frac{1}{2}[H^T(x - a) + H(x - a)],$$

> because $\nabla(x^T A x) = A^T x + A x$ combined with the multivariable chain rule.

$$= \nabla f(a) + \frac{1}{2} \cdot 2H(x - a) \text{ because the Hessian is symmetric.}$$

$$= \nabla f(a) + H(x - a)$$

Setting $\nabla q(x) = 0$ $\implies$ $\nabla f(a) + H(x - a) = 0$

$\implies$ $H(x - a) = -\nabla f(a)$

$\implies$ $x - a = -H^{-1}\nabla f(a)$ assuming H is invertible.

$\implies$ $x = a - H^{-1}\nabla f(a)$.

Thus, the maximum of $q(x)$ occurs at $x = a - H^{-1}\nabla f(a)$ assuming H is negative definite because $Hess(q) = H^T = H$.

Let $x_0 = a$ and

$$x_{t+1} = x_t - H^{-1}\nabla f(x_t), \qquad \text{where } H = \nabla^2 f(x_t), \text{ the Hessian of } f \text{ evaluated at } x_t.$$

By iteration, we get a sequence $x_0, x_1, x_2, \dots$ which should converge to the x-value that maximizes f.

To summarize the multivariate Newton-Raphson method:

Suppose $f: \mathbb{R}^k \longrightarrow \mathbb{R}$ is twice continuously differentiable.

1. Pick an initial value $x_0 = a$.
2. Let $x_{t+1} = x_t - H^{-1}\nabla f(x_t)$, where $H = \nabla^2 f(x_t)$.
3. f attains a max at the x-value to which the sequence $\{x_0, x_1, \dots\}$ converges.

MAXIMIZING THE LOG-LIKELIHOOD FUNCTION

We now return to maximizing $L(\beta)$.

Recall $L(\beta) = \sum_{i=1}^{N} \left[y_i \beta^T z_i' - \log\left(1 + e^{\beta^T z_i'}\right) \right]$.

Note that $L(\beta)$ is a real-valued function of $\beta = (\beta_0, \beta_1, \dots, \beta_p)$. So L is a function from $\mathbb{R}^{p+1}$ to $\mathbb{R}$. Further, L is twice continuously differentiable. So we can apply the multivariate Newton-Raphson method.

1. Pick an initial value $\beta^{(0)} = (a_0, a_1, \dots, a_p)$.
2. Let $\beta^{(t+1)} = \beta^{(t)} - H^{-1}\nabla L(\beta^{(t)})$, where $H = \nabla^2 L(\beta^{(t)})$.
3. L attains a max at the β-value to which the sequence $\{\beta^{(0)}, \beta^{(1)}, \dots\}$ converges.

To apply the Newton-Raphson method, we need to find the gradient of L and the Hessian of L.

Recall $L(\beta) = \sum_{i=1}^{N} \left[y_i \beta^T z_i' - \log\left(1 + e^{\beta^T z_i'}\right) \right]$.

$$\nabla L(\beta) = \frac{\partial L(\beta)}{\partial \beta} = \begin{bmatrix} \frac{\partial L(\beta)}{\partial \beta_0} \\ \vdots \\ \frac{\partial L(\beta)}{\partial \beta_p} \end{bmatrix}. \text{ Note } \frac{\partial L(\beta)}{\partial \beta_j} = \sum_{i=1}^{N} \frac{\partial}{\partial \beta_j} \left[y_i \beta^T z_i' - log\left(1 + e^{\beta^T z_i'}\right) \right]$$

$$= \sum_{i=1}^{N} \left[y_i z_{ij} - \frac{1}{1+e^{\beta^T z_i'}} \cdot e^{\beta^T z_i'} \cdot z_{ij} \right]$$

$$= \sum_{i=1}^{N} z_{ij} \left(y_i - \frac{e^{\beta^T z_i'}}{1+e^{\beta^T z_i'}} \right)$$

$$= \sum_{i=1}^{N} z_{ij} (y_i - p(z_i; \beta))$$

$$\Rightarrow \quad \nabla L(\beta) = \begin{bmatrix} \sum_{i=1}^{N} z_{i0}(y_i - p(z_i; \beta)) \\ \sum_{i=1}^{N} z_{i1}(y_i - p(z_i; \beta)) \\ \vdots \\ \sum_{i=1}^{N} z_{ip}(y_i - p(z_i; \beta)) \end{bmatrix}$$

$$= \sum_{i=1}^{N} \begin{bmatrix} z_{i0}(y_i - p(z_i; \beta)) \\ z_{i1}(y_i - p(z_i; \beta)) \\ \vdots \\ z_{ip}(y_i - p(z_i; \beta)) \end{bmatrix}$$

$$= \sum_{i=1}^{N} \begin{bmatrix} z_{i0} \\ z_{i1} \\ \vdots \\ z_{ip} \end{bmatrix} (y_i - p(z_i; \beta))$$

$$= \sum_{i=1}^{N} z_i'(y_i - p(z_i; \beta))$$

Thus, $\nabla L(\beta) = \sum_{i=1}^{N} z_i'(y_i - p(z_i; \beta))$.

Now, for the Hessian:

$$H = \nabla^2 L(\beta) = (a_{tj}) \text{ where } a_{tj} = \frac{\partial}{\partial \beta_t} \frac{\partial L(\beta)}{\partial \beta_j}.$$

From earlier, we know $\frac{\partial L(\beta)}{\partial \beta_j} = \sum_{i=1}^{N} z_{ij} \left(y_i - \frac{e^{\beta^T z_i'}}{1+e^{\beta^T z_i'}} \right)$.

$$\Rightarrow \quad \frac{\partial}{\partial \beta_t} \frac{\partial L(\beta)}{\partial \beta_j} = \frac{\partial}{\partial \beta_t} \sum_{i=1}^{N} z_{ij} \left(y_i - \frac{e^{\beta^T z_i'}}{1+e^{\beta^T z_i'}} \right)$$

$$= \sum_{i=1}^{N} z_{ij} \left(-\frac{\left(1+e^{\beta^T z_i'}\right)\left(e^{\beta^T z_i'} \cdot z_{it}\right) - e^{\beta^T z_i'} \cdot e^{\beta^T z_i'} \cdot z_{it}}{\left(1+e^{\beta^T z_i'}\right)^2} \right) \quad \text{by quotient rule}$$

$$= \sum_{i=1}^{N} z_{ij} \left(-\frac{e^{\beta^T z_i'} + e^{2\beta^T z_i'} \cdot z_{it} - e^{2\beta^T z_i'} \cdot z_{it}}{\left(1 + e^{\beta^T z_i'}\right)^2} \right)$$

$$= \sum_{i=1}^{N} z_{ij} \left(-\frac{e^{\beta^T z_i'} \cdot z_{it}}{\left(1 + e^{\beta^T z_i'}\right)^2} \right)$$

$$= -\sum_{i=1}^{N} z_{ij} \left(\frac{e^{\beta^T z_i'} \cdot z_{it}}{\left(1 + e^{\beta^T z_i'}\right)} \right) \cdot \frac{1}{\left(1 + e^{\beta^T z_i'}\right)}$$

$$= -\sum_{i=1}^{N} z_{ij} z_{it} \left(\frac{e^{\beta^T z_i'}}{\left(1 + e^{\beta^T z_i'}\right)} \right) \cdot \frac{1}{\left(1 + e^{\beta^T z_i'}\right)}$$

$$= -\sum_{i=1}^{N} z_{ij} z_{it} \cdot p(z_i; \beta) \cdot (1 - p(z_i; \beta))$$

$$\Longrightarrow \qquad \frac{\partial}{\partial \beta_t} \frac{\partial L(\beta)}{\partial \beta_j} = -\sum_{i=1}^{N} z_{ij} z_{it} \cdot p(z_i; \beta) \cdot (1 - p(z_i; \beta))$$

$$\Longrightarrow \qquad \nabla^2 L(\beta) = -\sum_{i=1}^{N} z_i'(z_i')^T p(z_i; \beta)(1 - p(z_i; \beta))$$

We can express the gradient $\nabla L(\beta)$ and the Hessian $\nabla^2 L(\beta)$ in matrix notation as follows:

Let $\boldsymbol{y} = \begin{bmatrix} y_1 \\ \vdots \\ y_N \end{bmatrix}$,

$$Z = \begin{bmatrix} z_{10} & z_{11} & \cdots & z_{1p} \\ \vdots & & & \\ z_{N0} & z_{N1} & \cdots & z_{Np} \end{bmatrix}, \qquad \text{(the rows of } Z \text{ consist of the } z_i''\text{s.)}$$

$$\boldsymbol{p} = \begin{bmatrix} p(z_1; \beta) \\ \vdots \\ p(z_N; \beta) \end{bmatrix}, \text{ and}$$

$$W = \begin{bmatrix} p(z_1; \beta)(1 - p(z_1; \beta)) & \cdots & 0 \\ \vdots & \ddots & \vdots \\ 0 & \cdots & p(z_N; \beta)(1 - p(z_N; \beta)) \end{bmatrix}.$$

Then, $\nabla L(\beta) = \sum_{i=1}^{N} z_i'(y_i - p(z_i; \beta)) = Z^T(\boldsymbol{y} - \boldsymbol{p})$.

$$\nabla^2 L(\beta) = -\sum_{i=1}^{N} z_i'(z_i')^T p(z_i; \beta)\big(1 - p(z_i; \beta)\big) = -Z^T W Z.$$

So, in the Newton-Raphson method,

$\beta^{(t+1)} = \beta^{(t)} - H^{-1}\nabla L(\beta^{(t)})$, where $H = \nabla^2 L(\beta^{(t)})$

$$= \beta^{(t)} - (-Z^T W Z)^{-1} Z^T (\boldsymbol{y} - \boldsymbol{p}) \quad \text{where we substitute } \beta = \beta^{(t)} \text{ in } \boldsymbol{p} \text{ and } W.$$

$$= \beta^{(t)} + (Z^T W Z)^{-1} Z^T (\boldsymbol{y} - \boldsymbol{p})$$

$$= (Z^T W Z)^{-1}(Z^T W Z)\beta^{(t)} + (Z^T W Z)^{-1} Z^T (\boldsymbol{y} - \boldsymbol{p})$$

$$= (Z^T W Z)^{-1}(Z^T W)(Z\beta^{(t)}) + (Z^T W Z)^{-1} Z^T W W^{-1}(\boldsymbol{y} - \boldsymbol{p})$$

$$= (Z^T W Z)^{-1}(Z^T W)(Z\beta^{(t)}) + (Z^T W Z)^{-1} Z^T W (W^{-1}(\boldsymbol{y} - \boldsymbol{p}))$$

$$= (Z^T W Z)^{-1}(Z^T W)\left[(Z\beta^{(t)} + W^{-1}(\boldsymbol{y} - \boldsymbol{p})\right]$$

$$= (Z^T W Z)^{-1}(Z^T W)\boldsymbol{v} \quad \text{where } \boldsymbol{v} = Z\beta^{(t)} + W^{-1}(\boldsymbol{y} - \boldsymbol{p})$$

So we can write the iterative step in the Newton-Raphson method as:

$$\beta^{(t+1)} = (Z^T W Z)^{-1}(Z^T W)\boldsymbol{v} \quad \text{where } \boldsymbol{v} = Z\beta^{(t)} + W^{-1}(\boldsymbol{y} - \boldsymbol{p}).$$

This method is then called ***iterative reweighted least squares***. At each iteration, $\beta^{(t)}$ gets updated, and so do $\boldsymbol{p}$, W, and $\boldsymbol{v}$.

EXAMPLE: LOGISTIC REGRESSION

Suppose we have a set of data $(z_1 y_1), \dots, (z_5, y_5)$ as follows:

$z_1 = (1,3), z_2 = (2,4), z_3 = (4,1), z_4 = (3,1), z_5 = (4,2)$ with

$y_1 = y_2 = y_3 = k_0 = 0$ and $y_4 = y_5 = k_1 = 1$.

Apply logistic regression by doing the following:

a) Find the log-likelihood function $L(\beta)$.

b) Apply iterative reweighted least squares to find estimates for $\beta_0, \beta_1, \beta_2$.

c) Find the estimated probability function $\hat{p}(x)$, where $p(x) = \Pr(Y = 1 | X = x)$.

d) Classify the new point $x = (5,0)$ using $\hat{p}(x)$.

Solution:

a) The log-likelihood function $L(\beta)$ is given by

$$L(\beta) = \sum_{i=1}^{N} \left[y_i \beta^T z_i' - log(1 + e^{\beta^T z_i'}) \right]$$

$$= \sum_{i=1}^{5} \left[y_i \beta^T z_i' - log(1 + e^{\beta^T z_i'}) \right] \qquad \text{where } \beta = (\beta_0, \beta_1, \beta_2) \text{ and } z_i' = \begin{bmatrix} 1 \\ z_{i1} \\ z_{i2} \end{bmatrix}$$

$$= -log(1 + e^{\beta_0 + \beta_1 + 3\beta_2}) - log(1 + e^{\beta_0 + 2\beta_1 + 4\beta_2}) - log(1 + e^{\beta_0 + 4\beta_1 + \beta_2})$$
$$+ \beta_0 + 3\beta_1 + \beta_2 - log(1 + e^{\beta_0 + 3\beta_1 + \beta_2}) + \beta_0 + 4\beta_1 + 2\beta_2 - log(1 + e^{\beta_0 + 4\beta_1 + 2\beta_2})$$

b) In iterative reweighted least squares, we pick an initial value $\beta^{(0)}$ and update $\beta^{(t)}$ by

$$\beta^{(t+1)} = (Z^T W Z)^{-1} (Z^T W) v \quad \text{where } Z = \begin{bmatrix} 1 & 1 & 3 \\ 1 & 2 & 4 \\ 1 & 4 & 1 \\ 1 & 3 & 1 \\ 1 & 4 & 2 \end{bmatrix}, y = \begin{bmatrix} 0 \\ 0 \\ 0 \\ 1 \\ 1 \end{bmatrix}, p = \begin{bmatrix} p(z_1; \beta) \\ \vdots \\ p(z_5; \beta) \end{bmatrix},$$

$$W = \begin{bmatrix} p(z_1; \beta)(1 - p(z_1; \beta)) & \cdots & 0 \\ \vdots & \ddots & \vdots \\ 0 & \cdots & p(z_5; \beta)(1 - p(z_5; \beta)) \end{bmatrix}, \text{ and } v = Z\beta^{(t)} + W^{-1}(y - p)$$

Recall that $\left(z_i; \beta^{(t)} \right) = \dfrac{e^{\left(\beta^{(t)} \right)^T z_i'}}{1 + e^{\left(\beta^{(t)} \right)^T z_i'}}.$

We'll pick **0** as the initial value $\beta^{(0)}$.

Then, $p = \begin{bmatrix} 1/2 \\ 1/2 \\ 1/2 \\ 1/2 \\ 1/2 \end{bmatrix}, W = \begin{bmatrix} 1/4 & \cdots & 0 \\ \vdots & \ddots & \vdots \\ 0 & \cdots & 1/4 \end{bmatrix}, v = \begin{bmatrix} -2 \\ -2 \\ -2 \\ 2 \\ 2 \end{bmatrix}$

$$\Rightarrow \qquad \beta^{(1)} = \begin{bmatrix} -20/29 \\ 14/29 \\ -14/29 \end{bmatrix} \approx \begin{bmatrix} -.69 \\ .48 \\ -.48 \end{bmatrix}$$

We update p, W, v, and calculate $\beta^{(2)}$.

$$\beta^{(2)} \approx \begin{bmatrix} -.974 \\ .61 \\ -.61 \end{bmatrix}$$

If we keep iterating, we get

$$\beta^{(3)} \approx \begin{bmatrix} -1.046 \\ .641 \\ -.641 \end{bmatrix}$$

$$\beta^{(4)} \approx \begin{bmatrix} -1.05 \\ .642 \\ -.642 \end{bmatrix}$$

$\beta^{(5)}$ and $\beta^{(6)}$ are nearly the same as $\beta^{(4)}$. So, $\beta^{(t)}$ converges to $\begin{bmatrix} -1.05 \\ .642 \\ -.642 \end{bmatrix}$. The estimates

for $\beta_0, \beta_1, \beta_2$ are $\widehat{\beta_0} = -1.05, \widehat{\beta_1} = 0.642, \widehat{\beta_2} = -.0642$.

c) The estimated probability function $\hat{p}(x)$ is given by $\hat{p}(x) = \frac{e^{\widehat{\beta_0}+\widehat{\beta_1}x_1+\widehat{\beta_2}x_2}}{1+e^{\widehat{\beta_0}+\widehat{\beta_1}x_1+\widehat{\beta_2}x_2}}$.

So $\hat{p}(x) = \frac{e^{-1.05+0.642x_1-0.642x_2}}{1+e^{-1.05+0.642x_1-0.642x_2}}$.

d) $\hat{p}(5,0) = 0.8966$. Since there are only two classes, we classify x as of class 1 if $\hat{p}(x) > 1/2$. Therefore, we classify $(5,0)$ as of class 1. Note that setting $\widehat{\beta_0} + \widehat{\beta_1}x_1 + \widehat{\beta_2}x_2$ to 0 gives us a decision boundary that corresponds to $\hat{p}(x) = 1/2$. In this example, the decision boundary is given by $-1.05 + 0.642x_1 - 0.642x_2 = 0$. This is the line $x_2 = x_1 - 1.6$. Here is what it looks like with the data points:

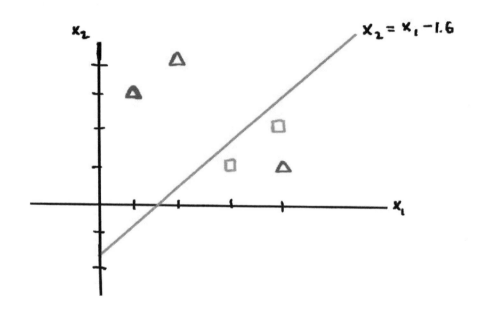

The inequality $x_2 > x_1 - 1.6$ corresponds to $\hat{p}(x) < 1/2$, and the inequality $x_2 < x_1 - 1.6$ corresponds to $\hat{p}(x) > 1/2$.

SUMMARY: LOGISTIC REGRESSION

- In logistic regression, we estimate $\Pr(Y = k \mid X = x)$ and pick the class k for which this probability is largest.

- We estimate $\Pr(Y = k \mid X = x)$ directly by assuming that the log-odds $\log\frac{p(x)}{1-p(x)}$ is a linear function of the components of x. That is, $\log\frac{p(x)}{1-p(x)} = \beta_0 + \beta_1 x_1 + \cdots + \beta_p x_p$ where $x = \begin{bmatrix} x_1 \\ \vdots \\ x_p \end{bmatrix}$.

- We find estimates for the parameters $\beta_0, \ldots, \beta_p$ by maximizing the log-likelihood function $L(\beta)$.

- We maximize the log-likelihood function $L(\beta)$ using the method of iterative reweighted least squares.

- Once we have estimates $\widehat{\beta_0}, \ldots, \widehat{\beta_p}$, we find the estimated probability function $\hat{p}(x)$.

- Using $\hat{p}(x)$, we can classify any new points.

PROBLEM SET: LOGISTIC REGRESSION

1. Suppose we have a set of data $(z_1, y_1), \ldots, (z_5, y_5)$ as follows:

   $z_1 = (1, 2), z_2 = (2, 1), z_3 = (2, 3), z_4 = (3, 2), z_5 = (1, 1)$ with

   $y_1 = y_2 = k_0 = 0$ and $y_3 = y_4 = y_5 = k_1 = 1$.

   Apply logistic regression by doing the following:

   a) Find the log-likelihood function $L(\beta)$.

   b) Apply iterative reweighted least squares to find estimates for $\beta_0, \beta_1, \beta_2$.

   c) Find the estimated probability function $\hat{p}(x)$, where $p(x) = \Pr(Y = 1 | X = x)$.

   d) Classify the new point $x = (1.5, 1)$ using $\hat{p}(x)$.

SOLUTION SET: LOGISTIC REGRESSION

1. a) The log-likelihood function $L(\beta)$ is given by

$$L(\beta) = \sum_{i=1}^{N}[y_i \beta^T z_i' - \log(1 + e^{\beta^T z_i'})]$$

$$
\begin{aligned}
= &-\log\left(1 + e^{\beta_0 + \beta_1 + 2\beta_2}\right) - \log\left(1 + e^{\beta_0 + 2\beta_1 + \beta_2}\right) \\
&+ \beta_0 + 2\beta_1 + 3\beta_2 - \log\left(1 + e^{\beta_0 + 2\beta_1 + 3\beta_2}\right) \\
&+ \beta_0 + 3\beta_1 + 2\beta_2 - \log\left(1 + e^{\beta_0 + 3\beta_1 + 2\beta_2}\right) \\
&+ \beta_0 + \beta_1 + \beta_2 - \log\left(1 + e^{\beta_0 + \beta_1 + \beta_2}\right)
\end{aligned}
$$

b) In iterative reweighted least squares, we pick an initial value $\beta^{(0)}$ and update $\beta^{(t)}$ by

$$\beta^{(t+1)} = (Z^T W Z)^{-1} Z^T W v \quad \text{where}$$

$$
Z = \begin{bmatrix} 1 & 1 & 2 \\ 1 & 2 & 1 \\ 1 & 2 & 3 \\ 1 & 3 & 2 \\ 1 & 1 & 1 \end{bmatrix}, y = \begin{bmatrix} 0 \\ 0 \\ 1 \\ 1 \\ 1 \end{bmatrix}, p = \begin{bmatrix} p(z_1; \beta^{(t)}) \\ \cdot \\ \cdot \\ \cdot \\ p(z_5; \beta^{(t)}) \end{bmatrix},
$$

$$
W = \begin{bmatrix} p(z_1; \beta^{(t)})(1 - p(z_1; \beta^{(t)})) & \cdots & 0 \\ \vdots & \ddots & \vdots \\ 0 & \cdots & p(z_5; \beta^{(t)})(1 - p(z_5; \beta^{(t)})) \end{bmatrix},
$$

and $v = Z\beta^{(t)} + W^{-1}(y - p)$.

Recall that $\left(z_i; \beta^{(t)}\right) = \dfrac{e^{\left(\beta^{(t)}\right)^T z_i'}}{1 + e^{\left(\beta^{(t)}\right)^T z_i'}}$.

We'll pick $\mathbf{0}$ as the initial value $\beta^{(0)}$.

Then, $p = \begin{bmatrix} 1/2 \\ 1/2 \\ 1/2 \\ 1/2 \\ 1/2 \end{bmatrix}$, $W = \begin{bmatrix} 1/4 & \cdots & 0 \\ \vdots & \ddots & \vdots \\ 0 & \cdots & 1/4 \end{bmatrix}$, $v = \begin{bmatrix} -2 \\ -2 \\ 2 \\ 2 \\ 2 \end{bmatrix}$

$$\Rightarrow \quad \beta^{(1)} = \begin{bmatrix} -2 \\ 2/3 \\ 2/3 \end{bmatrix} \approx \begin{bmatrix} -2 \\ 0.667 \\ 0.667 \end{bmatrix}$$

We update p, W, v and calculate $\beta^{(2)}$.

$$\beta^{(2)} \approx \begin{bmatrix} -2.28 \\ 0.77 \\ 0.77 \end{bmatrix}.$$

If we keep iterating, we get

$$\beta^{(3)} \approx \begin{bmatrix} -2.3 \\ 0.778 \\ 0.778 \end{bmatrix}$$

$$\beta^{(4)} \approx \begin{bmatrix} -2.3 \\ 0.778 \\ 0.778 \end{bmatrix}$$

$\beta^{(5)}$ and $\beta^{(6)}$ are nearly the same as $\beta^{(4)}$. So, $\beta^{(t)}$ converges to $\begin{bmatrix} -2.3 \\ 0.778 \\ 0.778 \end{bmatrix}$.

The estimates for $\beta_0, \beta_1, \beta_2$ are $\widehat{\beta_0} = -2.3, \widehat{\beta_1} = 0.778, \widehat{\beta_2} = 0.778$.

c) The estimated probability function $\hat{p}(x)$ is given by $\hat{p}(x) = \frac{e^{\widehat{\beta_0}+\widehat{\beta_1}x_1+\widehat{\beta_2}x_2}}{1+e^{\widehat{\beta_0}+\widehat{\beta_1}x_1+\widehat{\beta_2}x_2}}.$

So $\hat{p}(x) = \frac{e^{-2.3+0.778x_1+0.778x_2}}{1+e^{-2.3+0.778x_1+0.778x_2}}.$

d) $\hat{p}(1.5, 1) = 0.412$. We classify x as of class 1 if $\hat{p}(x) > 1/2$ and as of class 0 if $\hat{p}(x) < 1/2$.

Therefore, we classify $(1.5, 1)$ as of class 0. The decision boundary is given by

$$-2.3 + 0.778x_1 + 0.778x_2 = 0.$$

This is the line $x_2 = -x_1 + 2.956$.

Here is what it looks like with the data points:

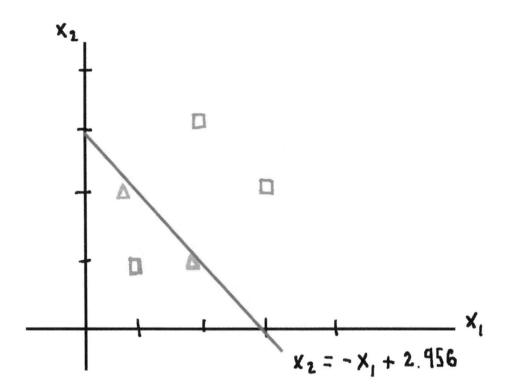

$x_2 > -x_1 + 2.956$ corresponds to $\hat{p}(x) > 1/2$, and

$x_2 < -x_1 + 2.956$ corresponds to $\hat{p}(x) < 1/2$.

5 – ARTIFICIAL NEURAL NETWORKS

ARTIFICIAL NEURAL NETWORKS

In this section, we'll look at a method for solving both regression and classification problems that uses certain compositions of linear and nonlinear functions. We construct functions involving unknown parameters that will give us the correct prediction or output value for any given input. The goal, then, would be to find the unknown parameters that minimize error using our training data. The functions we construct can be represented by a network diagram.

NEURAL NETWORK MODEL OF THE OUTPUT FUNCTIONS

Suppose $X_1, ..., X_p$ are some input variables. We can represent these as follows:

We'll call these 'input units', and together they form the 'input layer' of the neural network.

We include one additional input unit consisting of the constant 1:

This additional input unit is called a **bias unit**.

Now, suppose we take a linear combination of the input units $\alpha_0 \cdot 1 + \alpha_1 X_1 + \cdots + \alpha_p X_p$.

Letting $\alpha = (\alpha_0, \alpha_1, \ldots, \alpha_p)$ and $X = (1, X_1, \ldots, X_p)$, we can rewrite the linear combination as $\alpha^T X$. Such a linear combination is called an **activation**.

Suppose we then took $h(\alpha^T X)$, where h is a differentiable (possibly nonlinear) function. h is called an **activation function**.

Suppose we form M such activations $a_i = \alpha_i^T X$ where $\alpha_i = (\alpha_{i0}, \alpha_{i1}, \ldots, \alpha_{ip})$ and $i = 1, \ldots, M$.

Taking h of each activation a_i, we get $Z_i = h(\alpha_i^T X)$ for $i = 1, \ldots, M$.

We can represent the Z_i as follows:

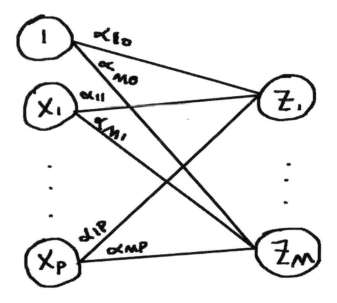

The Z_i are called **hidden units**, and together they form the **hidden layer** of the neural network. The $\alpha_{ij}'s$ are called **weights**.

Again, we include one additional hidden unit consisting of the constant 1:

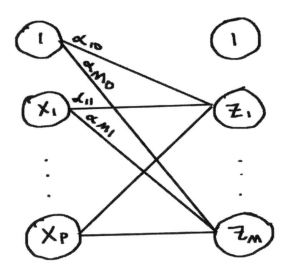

We could continue this process of creating more and more hidden layers, but we won't for now.

Now, suppose we take a linear combination of the hidden units $\beta_0 \cdot 1 + \beta_1 Z_1 + \cdots + \beta_M Z_M$. Letting $\beta = (\beta_0, \beta_1, \ldots, \beta_M)$ and $Z = (1, Z_1, \ldots, Z_M)$, we can rewrite the linear combination as $\beta^T Z$.

Suppose we form K such activations $b_k = \beta_k^T Z$ where $\beta_k = (\beta_{k0}, \beta_{k1}, \ldots, \beta_{kM})$ and $k = 1, \ldots, K$.

Suppose, for a fixed k, we applied some activation function g_k to the vector of activations $(b_1, \ldots, b_K)$ to get $Y_k = g_k(b_1, \ldots, b_K)$. Suppose we have such activation functions g_k for each $k = 1, \ldots, K$ and that we defined Y_k in the same way.

We can represent the Y_k as follows:

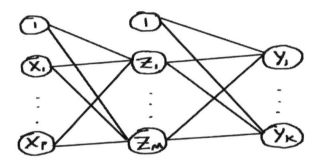

The Y_k are called **output units**, and together they form the **output layer** of the neural network.

Writing out $Y_k = g_k(b_1, \ldots, b_K)$ more explicitly, we get

$$Y_k = g_k(b_1, \ldots, b_K) \text{ where } b_k = \beta_{k0} + \sum_{i=1}^{M} \beta_{ki} Z_i$$

$$= \sum_{i=0}^{M} \beta_{ki} Z_i \text{ if we let } Z_0 = 1$$

$$= \sum_{i=0}^{M} \beta_{ki} h(\alpha_i^T X) \text{ if we let } h(\alpha_0^T X) = 1$$

$$= \sum_{i=0}^{M} \beta_{ki} h\left(\alpha_{i0} + \sum_{j=1}^{p} \alpha_{ij} X_j \right)$$

$$= \sum_{i=0}^{M} \beta_{ki} h\left(\sum_{j=0}^{p} \alpha_{ij} X_j \right) \text{ if we let } X_0 = 1$$

So b_k can be seen as a composition of linear functions (the linear combinations) and possibly nonlinear functions in an alternating fashion. More explicitly, we're taking linear combinations of $X_1, \ldots, X_p$ and of the bias unit X_0 and applying the activation function h to them to get $Z_1, \ldots, Z_M$. We're then taking linear combinations of $Z_1, \ldots, Z_M$ and of the bias unit Z_0 and applying the activation function g_k to the collection of all of them to get Y_k.

The network diagram we constructed has a single hidden layer, and the corresponding neural network model is called a ***single layer perceptron***. If there are multiple hidden layers, the corresponding neural network model is called a ***multilayer perceptron***.

FORWARD PROPAGATION

If the weights and activation functions are given and we feed values in for the input units $X_1, \ldots, X_p$ in the network diagram, we can calculate the values for the hidden units and, from there, the output units. In the diagram, we're moving from left to right starting with the input layer, moving on to the hidden layer or hidden layers, and arriving at the output layer. Such a movement of information is called *forward propagation*.

CHOOSING ACTIVATION FUNCTIONS

So how are neural network models used to solve regression and classification problems? Depending on the type of problem, different activation functions are used. Usually, the activation function h is chosen to be the logistic sigmoid function or the $tanh$ function.

For a regression problem, the output unit activation function g_k is typically chosen to be the kth projection for each k so that $Y_k = g_k(b_1, \ldots, b_K)$

$$= \pi_k(b_1, \ldots, b_K)$$

$$= b_k$$

This makes sense for a regression problem since b_k is a linear combination of the Z_i and can potentially take on any real value.

For a binary classification problem, the output unit activation function g_k is typically chosen to be the logistic sigmoid function of the kth projection function for each k so that

$$Y_k = g_k(b_1, \ldots, b_K)$$

$$= \sigma(\pi_k(b_1, \ldots, b_K))$$

$$= \sigma(b_k) \text{ where } \sigma(u) = \frac{1}{1+e^{-u}}$$

The graph of σ looks like this:

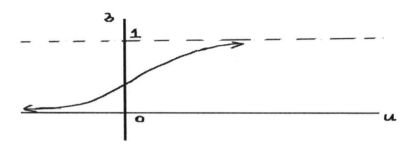

So $Y_k = \sigma(b_k)$ is between 0 and 1. This makes sense for a binary classification problem. Y_k can be interpreted as the probability that X is of class 1, and $1 - Y_k$ can be interpreted as the probability that X is of class 0.

For a K-class classification problem, the output unit activation function g_k is typically chosen to be the kth projection of the softmax function so that

$$Y_k = g_k(b_1, \dots, b_K)$$

$$= \pi_k\big(g(b_1, \dots, b_K)\big),$$

where g is the softmax function given by $g(a_1, \dots, a_m) = \left(\frac{e^{a_1}}{\sum_{i=1}^{m} e^{a_i}}, \dots, \frac{e^{a_m}}{\sum_{i=1}^{m} e^{a_i}} \right)$

$$= \pi_k \left(\frac{e^{b_1}}{\sum_{i=1}^{K} e^{b_i}}, \dots, \frac{e^{b_K}}{\sum_{i=1}^{K} e^{b_i}} \right)$$

$$= \frac{e^{b_k}}{\sum_{i=1}^{K} e^{b_i}}$$

This makes sense since each Y_k is between 0 and 1, and $\sum_{k=1}^{K} Y_k = 1$. Y_k can be interpreted as the probability that X is of class k.

ESTIMATING THE OUTPUT FUNCTIONS

So far, we've constructed output values Y_k that depend on an input x and that involve a bunch of unknown parameters. Our goal now is to use our training data to find values for the unknown parameters that minimize error. Recall that, in our network diagram, we had unknown parameters α_{ij} where $i = 1, ..., M$ and $j = 0, ..., p$ and β_{kl} where $k = 1, ..., K$ and $l = 0, ..., M$. We called these weights. We'll form the vector consisting of all these weights and denote it by $\boldsymbol{w}$.

For each type of problem, whether regression, binary classification, or multiclass classification, we're going to use a different error function. The error function $E(\boldsymbol{w})$ will turn out to be a sum of error functions $E_n(\boldsymbol{w})$, where $n = 1, ..., N$ and N is the number of training points. Let $\{(x_n, t_{nk}) | n = 1, ..., N \text{ and } k = 1, ..., K\}$ be the set of training data.

$E(\boldsymbol{w}) = \sum_{n=1}^{N} E_n(\boldsymbol{w})$ where $E_n(\boldsymbol{w})$ will depend on the type of problem.

ERROR FUNCTION FOR REGRESSION

Let's look at regression first. The training data will consist of pairs (x_n, t_{nk}) where $t_{nk} \in \mathbb{R}$ and $n = 1, ..., N$ and $k = 1, ..., K$.

In our neural network model, we're going to use Y_k to model the kth response for input x. Let $f_k(x)$ be Y_k as defined by the neural network model with input x.

We want to find the set of weights that minimizes the sum-of-squares error function

$E(\boldsymbol{w}) = \sum_{n=1}^{N} \sum_{k=1}^{K} (f_k(x_n) - t_{nk})^2$

This is analogous to minimizing the residual sum of squares in linear regression. Scaling the error function by $\frac{1}{2}$ doesn't make a difference in the minimization. So we can write

$E(\boldsymbol{w}) = \sum_{n=1}^{N} E_n(\boldsymbol{w})$ where $E_n(\boldsymbol{w}) = \frac{1}{2}\sum_{k=1}^{K}(f_k(x_n) - t_{nk})^2$.

We do this for computational convenience. $E(\boldsymbol{w})$ is called the ***sum-of-squares error function***.

ERROR FUNCTION FOR BINARY CLASSIFICATION

Next, let's look at binary classification. The training data will consist of pairs (x_n, t_{nk}) where $t_{nk} \in \{0,1\}$ and $n = 1, \ldots, N$ and $k = 1, \ldots, K$. Let t_k be the output variables.

Let $p_k(x) = \Pr(t_k = 1 | X = x)$, the conditional probability that t_k is 1 given that the input variable X is x.

Let n be fixed.

The t_k values are either 0 or 1. The probability of the observed data for x_n is given by the product of the probabilities that $t_k = 1$ for those k such that $t_{nk} = 1$ and the probabilities that $t_k = 0$ for those k such that $t_{nk} = 0$. That is,

$$\prod_{k:t_{nk}=1} \Pr(t_k = 1 | X = x_n) \prod_{k:t_{nk}=0} \Pr(t_k = 0 | X = x_n)$$

Since $\Pr(t_k = 0 | X = x_n) = 1 - \Pr(t_k = 1 | X = x_n)$, we can rewrite the product as

$$\prod_{k:t_{nk}=1} Pr(t_k = 1 | X = x_n) \prod_{k:t_{nk}=0} 1 - Pr(t_k = 1 | X = x_n)$$

$$= \prod_{k:t_{nk}=1} p_k(x_n) \prod_{k:t_{nk}=0} (1 - p_k(x_n))$$

We can rewrite this as $\prod_{k=1}^{K}(p_k(x_n))^{t_{nk}}(1 - p_k(x_n))^{1-t_{nk}}$. This is the probability of the observed data for a fixed x_n. The probability of the observed data for all of the x_n's is

$$\prod_{n=1}^{N}\prod_{k=1}^{K}(p_k(x_n))^{t_{nk}}(1 - p_k(x_n))^{1-t_{nk}}$$

We want to maximize the probability of our observed data given by this product.

In our neural network model, we're going to use the Y_k's to model the conditional probabilities $p_k(x)$'s. Let $f_k(x)$ be Y_k as defined by the neural network model with input x.

In our product, replace $p_k(x_n)$ with $f_k(x_n)$ to get $\prod_{n=1}^{N}\prod_{k=1}^{K}(f_k(x_n))^{t_{nk}}(1 - f_k(x_n))^{1-t_{nk}}$. This is our likelihood function. We want to find the set of weights that maximizes the likelihood function.

Maximizing the likelihood function is equivalent to minimizing the negative log of the likelihood function. Taking negative log of the likelihood function, we get

$$-\sum_{n=1}^{N}\sum_{k=1}^{K}[t_{nk}\log f_k(x_n) + (1 - t_{nk})\log(1 - f_k(x_n))]$$

So $E(\boldsymbol{w}) = \sum_{n=1}^{N} E_n(\boldsymbol{w})$ where $E_n(\boldsymbol{w}) = -\sum_{k=1}^{K}[t_{nk}\log f_k(x_n) + (1 - t_{nk})\log(1 - f_k(x_n))]$. $E(\boldsymbol{w})$ is called the ***cross-entropy error function***.

ERROR FUNCTION FOR MULTI-CLASS CLASSIFICATION

Next, let's look at multi-class classification. The training data will consist of pairs (x_n, t_{nk}) where $t_{nk} \in \{0, 1\}$ and $n = 1, \dots, N$ and $k = 1, \dots, K$.

Let t_k be the output variables. Let $p_k(x) = \Pr(t_k = 1 | X = x)$, the conditional probability that t_k is 1 given that the input X is x.

Let n be fixed.

The t_k values are either 0 or 1; only one of the t_k values is 1, and the rest are 0. The probability of the observed data for x_n is given by the probability that $t_k = 1$ for that k such that $t_{nk} = 1$. That is, $\Pr(t_k = 1 | X = x_n)$. We can rewrite this as $p_k(x_n) = \prod_{k=1}^{K}(p_k(x_n))^{t_{nk}}$. This is the probability of the observed data for a fixed x_n. The probability of the observed data for all of the x_n's is

$$\prod_{n=1}^{N}\prod_{k=1}^{K}(p_k(x_n))^{t_{nk}}$$

We want to maximize the probability of our observed data given by this product.

In our neural network model, we're going to use the Y_k's to model the conditional probabilities $p_k(x)$'s. Let $f_k(x)$ be Y_k as defined by the neural network model with input x.

In our product, replace $p_k(x_n)$ with $f_k(x_n)$ to get $\prod_{n=1}^{N}\prod_{k=1}^{K}(f_k(x_n))^{t_{nk}}$. This is our likelihood function. We want to find the set of weights that maximizes the likelihood function. Maximizing the likelihood function is equivalent to minimizing the negative log of the likelihood function. Taking negative log of the likelihood function, we get

$$-\sum_{n=1}^{N}\sum_{k=1}^{K} t_{nk} \log f_k(x_n)$$

So $E(\boldsymbol{w}) = \sum_{n=1}^{N} E_n(\boldsymbol{w})$ where $E_n(\boldsymbol{w}) = -\sum_{k=1}^{K} t_{nk} \log f_k(x_n)$.

$E(\boldsymbol{w})$ is called the ***multi-class cross-entropy error function***.

MINIMIZING THE ERROR FUNCTION USING GRADIENT DESCENT

So far, we've seen that, for each type of problem, there is a corresponding error function $E(\boldsymbol{w})$. The method we use to minimize $E(\boldsymbol{w})$ is gradient descent.

Gradient descent is an iterative process where we start with an initial value for $\boldsymbol{w}$ and update $\boldsymbol{w}$ as follows:

$$\boldsymbol{w}^{(\tau+1)} = \boldsymbol{w}^{(\tau)} - \eta \nabla E(\boldsymbol{w}^{(\tau)})$$

η is called the ***learning rate***.

In the process of updating $\boldsymbol{w}$, we need to find the gradient of the error function.

$E(\boldsymbol{w})$ is a function of all the individual weights. Let w_{ji} denote the weight of the connection that goes from unit i to unit j, where unit i is the ith unit in some layer and unit j is the jth unit in the next layer.

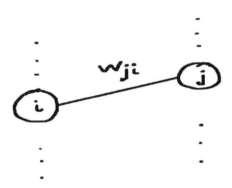

$\nabla E(\boldsymbol{w})$ is the vector consisting of all the partial derivatives $\frac{\partial E(\boldsymbol{w})}{\partial w_{ji}}$.

Since $E(\boldsymbol{w}) = \sum_{n=1}^{N} E_n(\boldsymbol{w})$, $\frac{\partial E(\boldsymbol{w})}{\partial w_{ji}} = \sum_{n=1}^{N} \frac{\partial E_n(\boldsymbol{w})}{\partial w_{ji}}$.

So we just need to calculate $\frac{\partial E_n(\boldsymbol{w})}{\partial w_{ji}}$ for each n.

Suppose l is a non-bias unit in the same layer as unit j. Recall that there is an activation a_l, corresponding to unit l, which is a linear combination of all of the units in the previous layer.

Note that $E_n(\boldsymbol{w})$ can be seen as a function of the activations a_l. By the multivariable chain rule, $\frac{\partial E_n(\boldsymbol{w})}{\partial w_{ji}} = \sum_l \frac{\partial E_n(\boldsymbol{w})}{\partial a_l} \cdot \frac{\partial a_l}{\partial w_{ji}}$, where l runs over all non-bias units in the same layer as unit j. However, a_l doesn't depend on w_{ji} unless $l = j$.

So $\frac{\partial a_l}{\partial w_{ji}} = 0 \ \forall l \neq j$.

$\implies \frac{\partial E_n(\boldsymbol{w})}{\partial w_{ji}} = \sum_l \frac{\partial E_n(\boldsymbol{w})}{\partial a_l} \cdot \frac{\partial a_l}{\partial w_{ji}} = \frac{\partial E_n(\boldsymbol{w})}{\partial a_j} \cdot \frac{\partial a_j}{\partial w_{ji}}$.

Now, $a_j = \sum_s w_{js} z_s$ where s runs over all units in the layer previous to the layer for unit j and z_s is the value for unit s.

$\implies \frac{\partial a_j}{\partial w_{ji}} = z_i$.

Thus, $\frac{\partial E_n(\boldsymbol{w})}{\partial w_{ji}} = \frac{\partial E_n(\boldsymbol{w})}{\partial a_j} \cdot z_i$.

Let $\delta_j \equiv \frac{\partial E_n(\boldsymbol{w})}{\partial a_j}$.

$\implies \frac{\partial E_n(\boldsymbol{w})}{\partial w_{ji}} = \delta_j z_i$.

BACKPROPAGATION EQUATIONS
It remains for us to find δ_j.

If j is an output unit k, then it can be shown that $\delta_k = f_k(x_n) - t_{nk}$. (You will show this in the practice problems)

Otherwise, j is a hidden unit. Note that we can view $E_n(\boldsymbol{w})$ as a function of the activations a_k

corresponding to the non-bias units k in the layer after the layer for unit j.

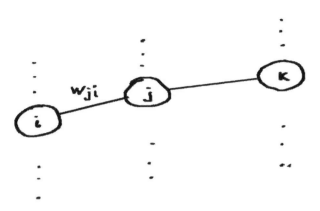

By the multivariable chain rule,

$$\delta_j = \frac{\partial E_n(\boldsymbol{w})}{\partial a_j} = \sum_k \frac{\partial E_n(\boldsymbol{w})}{\partial a_k} \cdot \frac{\partial a_k}{\partial a_j},$$

where k runs over all non-bias units in the layer after the layer for unit j.

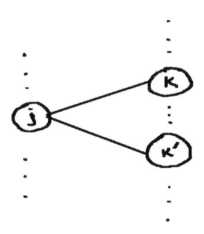

Now, $a_k = \sum_t w_{kt} h(a_t)$ where t runs over all units in the layer for j and h is some activation function.

$$\Longrightarrow \frac{\partial a_k}{\partial a_j} = w_{kj} h'(a_j).$$

Letting $\delta_k \equiv \frac{\partial E_n(w)}{\partial a_k}$, we get

$$\delta_j = \sum_k \delta_k w_{kj} h'(a_j)$$

$$= h'(a_j) \sum_k w_{kj} \delta_k$$

So δ_j is determined by the δ_k's for all those units k for which there is a connection that goes from unit j to unit k. The equations $\delta_j = h'(a_j) \sum_k w_{kj} \delta_k$ are called ***backpropagation equations***.

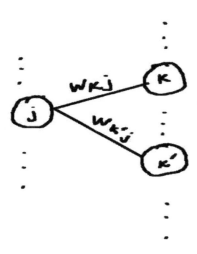

Information is propagated backwards from the units k to unit j, so to speak.

SUMMARY OF BACKPROPAGATION

To summarize, $\frac{\partial E(\boldsymbol{w})}{\partial w_{ji}} = \sum_{n=1}^{N} \frac{\partial E_n(\boldsymbol{w})}{\partial w_{ji}}$ where $\frac{\partial E_n(\boldsymbol{w})}{\partial w_{ji}} = \delta_j z_i$,

$$\delta_k = f_k(x_n) - t_{nk} \text{ if } k \text{ is an output unit, and}$$

$$\delta_j = h'(a_j) \sum_k w_{kj} \delta_k \text{ if } j \text{ is a hidden unit.}$$

We could find the δ_k's for all the output units k, then plug those into the backpropagation equations to find the δ_j's for all the hidden units j in the layer right before the output layer, then use these δ_j's to find the δ's in the next layer down, continuing in this way until we find all the δ's. This process of finding $\nabla E(\boldsymbol{w})$ is called **backpropagation**.

SUMMARY: ARTIFICIAL NEURAL NETWORKS

- We began by using a neural network diagram to construct output functions $f_k(x)$ for each output unit k.

- We used weights and activation functions to construct the output functions.

- We then used the training data and a chosen error function $E(w)$ to find values for the weights. We did this by minimizing the error function.

- For regression problems, we used the sum-of-squares error function along with the output activation function $g_k(b_1, \ldots, b_K) = b_k$.

- For binary classification problems, we used the cross-entropy error function along with the output activation function $g_k(b_1, \ldots, b_K) = \sigma(b_k)$, where σ is the logistic sigmoid function.

- For multiclass classification problems, we used the multiclass cross-entropy error function along with the output activation function $g_k(b_1, \ldots, b_K) = \frac{e^{b_k}}{\sum_{i=1}^{K} e^{b_i}}$, where $g_k = \pi_k \circ g$ and g is the softmax function.

- To minimize $E(w)$, we used gradient descent, which required finding $\nabla E(w^{(\tau)})$. To find $\nabla E(w^{(\tau)})$, we used backpropagation.

PROBLEM SET: ARTIFICIAL NEURAL NETWORKS

1. In the process of finding $\nabla E(\boldsymbol{w})$, we saw that $\frac{\partial E_n(\boldsymbol{w})}{\partial w_{ji}} = \delta_j z_i$, where $\delta_j \equiv \frac{\partial E_n(\boldsymbol{w})}{\partial a_j}$.

   Claim: If j is an output unit k, then $\delta_k = f_k(x_n) - t_{nk}$.

   a) Show the above claim holds for $E_n(\boldsymbol{w}) = \frac{1}{2}\sum_{k=1}^K (f_k(x_n) - t_{nk})^2$, corresponding to the sum-of-squares error function, where $f_k(x_n) = b_k$ (the activation for unit k).

   b) Show that the claim holds for

   $E_n(\boldsymbol{w}) = -\sum_{k=1}^K [t_{nk} \log f_k(x_n) + (1 - t_{nk}) \log(1 - f_k(x_n))]$, corresponding to the cross-entropy error function, where $f_k(x_n) = \sigma(b_k)$ with $\sigma(u) = \frac{1}{1+e^{-u}}$.

   c) Show that the claim holds for $E_n(\boldsymbol{w}) = -\sum_{k=1}^K t_{nk} \log f_k(x_n)$, corresponding to the multiclass cross-entropy error function, where $f_k(x_n) = \frac{e^{b_k}}{\sum_{i=1}^K e^{b_i}}$.

2. Consider a neural network with a single hidden layer used to solve a regression problem. Suppose the hidden unit activation function h is the logistic sigmoid function $h(u) = \frac{1}{1+e^{-u}}$ and the output unit activation function g_k is given by $g_k(b_1, \ldots, b_K) = b_k$ so that $Y_k = b_k$. Let the error function $E(\boldsymbol{w})$ be the sum-of-squares error function $E(\boldsymbol{w}) = \sum_{n=1}^N E_n(\boldsymbol{w})$, where $E_n(\boldsymbol{w}) = \sum_{k=1}^K (f_k(x_n) - t_{nk})^2$.

   a) Calculate $\delta_j \equiv \frac{\partial E_n(\boldsymbol{w})}{\partial a_j}$ for the case when j is an output unit and for the case when j is a hidden unit.

   b) Then calculate $\frac{\partial E_n(\boldsymbol{w})}{\partial w_{ji}}$ where w_{ji} is a weight for a connection going from the input layer to the hidden layer.

   c) Calculate $\frac{\partial E_n(\boldsymbol{w})}{\partial w_{kj}}$ where w_{kj} is a weight for a connection going from the hidden layer to the output layer.

SOLUTION SET: ARTIFICIAL NEURAL NETWORKS

1. a) If j is an output unit k, then $\delta_k = \frac{\partial E_n(\boldsymbol{w})}{\partial b_k}$ where b_k is the activation for unit k.

$$E_n(\boldsymbol{w}) = \frac{1}{2}\sum_{k=1}^{K}(f_k(x_n) - t_{nk})^2$$

$$= \frac{1}{2}\sum_{k=1}^{K}(b_k - t_{nk})^2$$

$\implies \frac{\partial E_n(\boldsymbol{w})}{\partial b_k} = \frac{1}{2}\frac{\partial(b_k - t_{nk})^2}{\partial b_k} = b_k - t_{nk} = f_k(x_n) - t_{nk}.$

$\implies \delta_k = f_k(x_n) - t_{nk}.$

b) If j is an output unit k, then $\delta_k = \frac{\partial E_n(\boldsymbol{w})}{\partial b_k}$ where b_k is the activation for unit k.

$$E_n(\boldsymbol{w}) = -\sum_{k=1}^{K}[t_{nk}\log f_k(x_n) + (1 - t_{nk})\log(1 - f_k(x_n))]$$

$$= -\sum_{k=1}^{K}[t_{nk}\log\sigma(b_k) + (1 - t_{nk})\log(1 - \sigma(b_k))]$$

$\implies \frac{\partial E_n(\boldsymbol{w})}{\partial b_k} = -\frac{\partial[t_{nk}\log\sigma(b_k) + (1 - t_{nk})\log(1 - \sigma(b_k))]}{\partial b_k}$

$= -[t_{nk}\frac{1}{\sigma(b_k)}\cdot\sigma'(b_k) + (1 - t_{nk})\cdot\frac{1}{1 - \sigma(b_k)}\cdot(-\sigma'(b_k))]$

$= -[t_{nk}\frac{1}{\sigma(b_k)}\cdot\sigma(b_k)(1 - \sigma(b_k)) + (1 - t_{nk})\cdot\frac{1}{1 - \sigma(b_k)}\cdot(-\sigma(b_k)\cdot(1 - \sigma(b_k)))]$

because $\sigma' = \sigma(1 - \sigma)$

$= -[t_{nk}(1 - \sigma(b_k)) + (1 - t_{nk})(-\sigma(b_k))]$

$= -[t_{nk} - \sigma(b_k)]$
$= \sigma(b_k) - t_{nk}$
$= f_k(x_n) - t_{nk}$

$\implies \delta_k = f_k(x_n) - t_{nk}.$

c) $E_n(\boldsymbol{w}) = -\sum_{k=1}^{K} t_{nk} \log f_k(x_n)$

$$= -\sum_{k=1}^{K} t_{nk} \log\left(\frac{e^{b_k}}{\sum_{i=1}^{K} e^{b_i}}\right)$$

$$\implies \frac{\partial E_n(\boldsymbol{w})}{\partial b_k} = \frac{\partial\left(-\sum_{j=1}^{K} t_{nj} \log\left(\frac{e^{b_j}}{\sum_{i=1}^{K} e^{b_i}}\right)\right)}{\partial b_k}$$

$$= -\sum_{j \neq k} t_{nj} \frac{\partial \log\left(\frac{e^{b_j}}{\sum_{i=1}^{K} e^{b_i}}\right)}{\partial b_k} - t_{nk} \frac{\partial \log\left(\frac{e^{b_k}}{\sum_{i=1}^{K} e^{b_i}}\right)}{\partial b_k}$$

$$= -\sum_{j \neq k} t_{nj} \frac{1}{f_j(x_n)} \cdot \left(-f_k(x_n) f_j(x_n)\right) - t_{nk} \cdot \frac{1}{f_k(x_n)} \cdot f_k(x_n)(1 - f_k(x_n))$$

$$= -\sum_{j \neq k} t_{nj}\left(-f_k(x_n)\right) - t_{nk}(1 - f_k(x_n))$$

$$= f_k(x_n) \sum_{j \neq k} t_{nj} + t_{nk} f_k(x_n) - t_{nk}$$

$$= f_k(x_n) \sum_{j} t_{nj} - t_{nk}$$

$$= f_k(x_n) - t_{nk} \quad \text{because } \sum_j t_{nj} = 1$$

$$\implies \delta_k = f_k(x_n) - t_{nk}$$

2. a) If j is an output unit k, then $\delta_k = \frac{\partial E_n(\boldsymbol{w})}{\partial b_k}$ where b_k is the activation for unit k. From problem 1, we already know $\delta_k = f_k(x_n) - t_{nk}$
$\implies \quad \delta_k = b_k - t_{nk}$.

If j is a hidden unit, then (by the backpropagation equations),

$\delta_j = h'(a_j) \sum_k w_{kj} \delta_k$ where k runs over all non-bias units in the layer after the layer for unit j.

$$= h(a_j)(1 - h(a_j)) \sum_k w_{kj} \delta_k \quad \text{because } h' = h(1 - h).$$

b) $\frac{\partial E_n(\boldsymbol{w})}{\partial w_{ji}} = \delta_j z_i$ where z_i is the value for unit i in the input layer.

Since j is a hidden unit, $\delta_j = h(a_j)(1 - h(a_j)) \sum_k w_{kj} \delta_k$.

c) $\frac{\partial E_n(w)}{\partial w_{kj}} = \delta_k z_j$ where z_j is the value for unit j in the hidden layer.

Since k is an output unit,

$$\delta_k = f_k(x_n) - t_{nk}$$

$$= b_k - t_{nk} \text{ where } b_k \text{ is the activation for unit } k.$$

6 – MAXIMAL MARGIN CLASSIFIER

MAXIMAL MARGIN CLASSIFIER

In this section, and in the next two sections, we will look at some further methods for solving classification problems. We will look at the maximal margin classifier, the support vector classifier, and the support vector machine. We will focus on the case of two classes labeled 1 and -1.

Suppose $(x_1, y_1), \ldots, (x_N, y_N)$ are our training data points. Each x_i is a p-dimensional vector $\begin{bmatrix} x_{i1} \\ \vdots \\ x_{ip} \end{bmatrix}$ and $y_i \in \{-1, 1\}$. For instance, if $p = 2$, the x_i are points in the two-dimensional plane. If we plot the points x_i, we might have something like this:

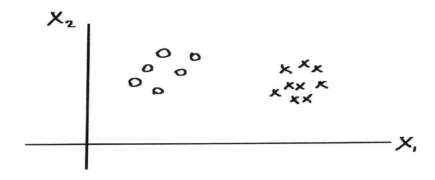

The circles indicate class 1 and the x's indicate class -1. In this example, the points appear to be separable by a line.

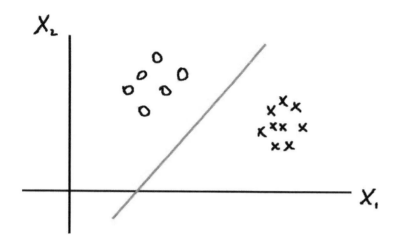

If the x_i's are separable like this by a line when $p = 2$, or by a hyperplane more generally, then we can use such a line to separate the two classes and classify any new point depending on which side of the line the point falls on. The maximal margin classifier is used in this case. If the x_i's can't be separated by a line (or hyperplane), we can still try to separate the two classes with a line (or hyperplane) using the support vector classifier. Finally, if we want a non-linear decision boundary separating the two classes, we can use the support vector machine.

DEFINITIONS OF SEPARATING HYPERPLANE AND MARGIN

First, let's start with the maximal margin classifier.

We want to define what a hyperplane is. The x_i's lie in $\mathbb{R}^p$, a p-dimensional vector space. A *hyperplane* in $\mathbb{R}^p$, for some constants $\beta_0, \dots, \beta_p$, is the set of points $(X_1, \dots, X_p)$ such that

$$\beta_0 + \beta_1 X_1 + \cdots + \beta_p X_p = 0.$$

If $p = 2$, a hyperplane in $\mathbb{R}^2$ is a line. If $p = 3$, a hyperplane in $\mathbb{R}^3$ is a plane.

Let's say that our x_i's are separable by a hyperplane. For instance,

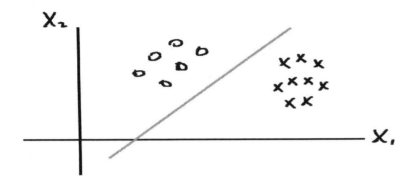

Note that there are multiple hyperplanes that separate our points.

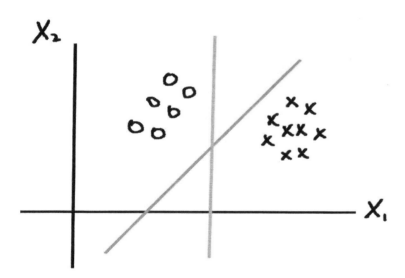

We want to choose our hyperplane such that the hyperplane is as far from each point as possible. Let's make this more precise.

A hyperplane $\beta_0 + \beta_1 X_1 + \cdots + \beta_p X_p = 0$ is said to be a *separating hyperplane* just in case

$\beta_0 + \beta_1 x_{i1} + \cdots + \beta_p x_{ip} > 0 \quad \text{if } y_i = 1$

$\beta_0 + \beta_1 x_{i1} + \cdots + \beta_p x_{ip} < 0 \quad \text{if } y_i = -1$

In other words, $y_i(\beta_0 + \beta_1 x_{i1} + \cdots + \beta_p x_{ip}) > 0$ for each $i = 1, \dots, N$.

It can be shown that the perpendicular distance between x_i and the separating hyperplane

$\beta_0 + \beta_1 X_1 + \cdots + \beta_p X_p = 0$ is given by $\frac{1}{\|\beta\|} \cdot y_i(\beta_0 + \beta_1 x_{i1} + \cdots + \beta_p x_{ip})$, where $\beta = (\beta_1, \dots, \beta_p)$. See Appendix 1 for the proof.

For a fixed separating hyperplane $\beta_0 + \beta_1 X_1 + \cdots + \beta_p X_p = 0$, consider the minimum distance between the x_i's and the separating hyperplane. In other words, consider

$$min\left\{\frac{1}{\|\beta\|} \cdot y_i(\beta_0 + \beta_1 x_{i1} + \cdots + \beta_p x_{ip}) \mid i = 1, \dots, N\right\}$$

This is the distance between the hyperplane and the x_i closest to the hyperplane. It's called the ***margin*** of the hyperplane.

MAXIMIZING THE MARGIN

We want to choose the separating hyperplane that maximizes the margin of the hyperplane. In other words, we want to choose $\beta_0, \beta_1, \dots, \beta_p$ such that the margin is maximal. So we have the following problem:

$$\begin{array}{c} maximize \\ (\beta_0, \beta_1, \dots, \beta_p) \in S \end{array} \quad min\left\{\frac{1}{\|\beta\|} \cdot y_i(\beta_0 + \beta_1 x_{i1} + \cdots + \beta_p x_{ip}) \mid i = 1, \dots, N\right\},$$

$$\text{where } S = \left\{(\beta_0, \beta_1, \dots, \beta_p) \in \mathbb{R}^{p+1} \mid y_i(\beta_0 + \beta_1 x_{i1} + \cdots + \beta_p x_{ip}) > 0 \; \forall i = 1, \dots, N\right\}$$

S should actually be the set

$$S_0 = \left\{(\beta_0, \beta_1, \dots, \beta_p) \in \mathbb{R}^{p+1} \mid y_i(\beta_0 + \beta_1 x_{i1} + \cdots + \beta_p x_{ip}) > 0 \; \forall i = 1, \dots, N \text{ and } \|\beta\| \neq 0\right\}$$

since we don't want $\|\beta\|$ to be 0.

However, we don't have to worry about this if we have at least two data points (x_i, y_i) and (x_j, y_j) in different classes. If $y_i \neq y_j$ for some pair (i, j), then assuming $\|\beta\| = 0$ implies that $(\beta_1, \dots, \beta_p) = \mathbf{0}$.

$\Rightarrow \; y_i(\beta_0) > 0$ and $y_j(\beta_0) > 0$

$\Rightarrow \; \beta_0$ is positive and negative, a contradiction.

So $S_0 = S$.

DEFINITION OF MAXIMAL MARGIN CLASSIFIER

Once we find $(\beta_0^*, \beta_1^*, \dots, \beta_p^*)$ that maximizes the margin, we can use the hyperplane given by $\beta_0^* + \beta_1^* X_1 + \cdots + \beta_p^* X_p = 0$ to classify a test point $(x_1, x_2, \dots, x_p)$ as follows:

If $\beta_0^* + \beta_1^* x_1 + \cdots + \beta_p^* x_p > 0$, then the test point is assigned to class 1.

If $\beta_0^* + \beta_1^* x_1 + \cdots + \beta_p^* x_p < 0$, then the test point is assigned to class -1.

This way of classifying test points is called the ***maximal margin classifier***.

REFORMULATING THE OPTIMIZATION PROBLEM

Now, let's see how the maximal margin hyperplane is found.

Letting $M_{\beta_0, \beta} = min\left\{\frac{1}{\|\beta\|} \cdot y_i(\beta_0 + \beta_1 x_{i1} + \cdots + \beta_p x_{ip}) \mid i = 1, \dots, N\right\}$,

we can reformulate the problem as:

$$\underset{(\beta_0, \beta) \in S}{maximize}\ M_{\beta_0, \beta}\ .$$

It turns out that the margin $M_{\beta_0, \beta}$ doesn't change if we multiply β_0 and β by some positive value k. That is, $M_{k\beta_0, k\beta} = M_{\beta_0, \beta}$. See Appendix 2 for the proof.

This fact allows us to impose the following condition:

$$min\{y_i(\beta_0 + \beta_1 x_{i1} + \cdots + \beta_p x_{ip}) \mid i = 1, \dots, N\} = 1$$

See Appendix 3 for the proof.

Thus, we can try to find a solution to our maximization problem that satisfies the condition to begin with by imposing the condition

$$min\{y_i(\beta_0 + \beta_1 x_{i1} + \cdots + \beta_p x_{ip}) \mid i = 1, \dots, N\} = 1$$

We now have the optimization problem:

$\underset{(\beta_0,\beta)\in S}{maximize} \, M_{\beta_0,\beta}$ given the condition

$$min\{y_i(\beta_0 + \beta_1 x_{i1} + \cdots + \beta_p x_{ip}) | i = 1, \ldots, N\} = 1.$$

Note that $M_{\beta_0,\beta} = \frac{1}{||\beta||} min\{y_i(\beta_0 + \beta_1 x_{i1} + \cdots + \beta_p x_{ip}) | i = 1, \ldots, N\}$

$$= \frac{1}{||\beta||} \cdot 1$$

$$= \frac{1}{||\beta||}$$

Maximizing $M_{\beta_0,\beta}$ is the same as minimizing $||\beta||$, which is equivalent to minimizing $\frac{1}{2}||\beta||^2$.

So our problem becomes: $\underset{(\beta_0,\beta)\in S}{minimize} \, \frac{1}{2}||\beta||^2$ given the constraint

$$min\{y_i(\beta_0 + \beta_1 x_{i1} + \cdots + \beta_p x_{ip}) | i = 1, \ldots, N\} = 1$$

Actually, we can relax the constraint by making it an inequality.

The problem (1) $\underset{(\beta_0,\beta)\in S}{minimize} \, \frac{1}{2}||\beta||^2$ given the constraint

$$min\{y_i(\beta_0 + \beta_1 x_{i1} + \cdots + \beta_p x_{ip}) | i = 1, \ldots, N\} = 1$$

is equivalent to

the problem (2) $\underset{(\beta_0,\beta)\in S}{minimize} \, \frac{1}{2}||\beta||^2$ given the constraint

$$min\{y_i(\beta_0 + \beta_1 x_{i1} + \cdots + \beta_p x_{ip}) | i = 1, \ldots, N\} \geq 1$$

in the sense that the first problem has a solution if and only if the second problem has a solution. See Appendix 4 for the proof.

Furthermore, the solutions to (1) and (2) will give the same value for $M_{\beta_0,\beta}$. See Appendix 5 for the proof.

We can, therefore, focus on solving the optimization problem

$\underset{(\beta_0,\beta)\in S}{minimize} \, \frac{1}{2}||\beta||^2$ given the constraint

$$min\{y_i(\beta_0 + \beta_1 x_{i1} + \cdots + \beta_p x_{ip}) | i = 1, \ldots, N\} \geq 1.$$

The constraint $min\{y_i(\beta_0 + \beta_1 x_{i1} + \cdots + \beta_p x_{ip}) | i = 1, \ldots, N\} \geq 1$ is equivalent to the constraint

$y_i(\beta_0 + \beta_1 x_{i1} + \cdots + \beta_p x_{ip}) \geq 1$ for $i = 1, \ldots, N$.

We can reformulate the optimization problem to be

$$\underset{(\beta_0,\beta)\in S}{minimize} \frac{1}{2}||\beta||^2 \quad \text{given the constraint}$$

$$y_i(\beta_0 + \beta_1 x_{i1} + \cdots + \beta_p x_{ip}) \geq 1 \text{ for } i = 1, \ldots, N.$$

The requirement that $(\beta_0, \beta) \in S$ is unnecessary because the constraint

$y_i(\beta_0 + \beta_1 x_{i1} + \cdots + \beta_p x_{ip}) \geq 1$ for $i = 1, \ldots, N$ implies that

$y_i(\beta_0 + \beta_1 x_{i1} + \cdots + \beta_p x_{ip}) > 0 \; \forall i = 1, \ldots, N.$

We can thus reformulate the optimization problem as:

$$\underset{(\beta_0,\beta)\in \mathbb{R}^{p+1}}{minimize} \frac{1}{2}||\beta||^2 \quad \text{given the constraint}$$

$$y_i(\beta_0 + \beta_1 x_{i1} + \cdots + \beta_p x_{ip}) \geq 1 \text{ for } i = 1, \ldots, N.$$

This is a convex optimization problem, where

$f : \mathbb{R}^{p+1} \rightarrow \mathbb{R}$ given by $f(\beta_0, \beta_1, \ldots, \beta_p) = \frac{1}{2}||\beta||^2$ and

$g_i : \mathbb{R}^{p+1} \rightarrow \mathbb{R}$ given by $g_i(\beta_0, \beta_1, \ldots, \beta_p) = 1 - y_i(\beta_0 + \cdots + \beta_p x_{ip})$, for $i = 1, \ldots, N,$

are differentiable convex functions.

Our convex optimization problem takes the form:

$$\underset{(\beta_0,\beta)\in \mathbb{R}^{p+1}}{minimize} f(\beta_0, \ldots, \beta_p) \quad \text{given the constraint}$$

$$g_i(\beta_0, \ldots, \beta_p) \leq 0 \text{ for } i = 1, \ldots, N.$$

SOLVING THE CONVEX OPTIMIZATION PROBLEM

We can solve this using Lagrange multipliers. Consider the Lagrangian $L : \mathbb{R}^{p+1} \times \mathbb{R}^N \rightarrow \mathbb{R}$ given by

$$L(x, \alpha) = f(x) + \sum_{i=1}^{N} \alpha_i g_i(x).$$

The α_i are called **Lagrange multipliers**.

KKT CONDITIONS

Our convex optimization problem has a solution $x^* = (\beta_0^*, \ldots, \beta_p^*)$ if there are Lagrange multipliers $\alpha_1^*, \ldots, \alpha_N^*$ such that the following conditions hold:

1. $g_i(x^*) \le 0$ for $i = 1, \dots, N$. (***primal feasibility***)
2. $\nabla_x L(x^*, \alpha^*) = 0$ where $\alpha^* = (\alpha_1^*, \dots, \alpha_N^*)$. (***Lagrangian stationarity***)
3. $\alpha_i^* \ge 0$ for $i = 1, \dots, N$. (***dual feasibility***)
4. $\alpha_i^* g_i(x^*) = 0$ for $i = 1, \dots, N$. (***complementary slackness***)

These conditions are called the ***KKT conditions***.

PRIMAL AND DUAL PROBLEMS

Consider the problem of finding $\displaystyle \min_{x} \ \max_{\alpha:\, \alpha_i \ge 0\ \forall i} L(x, \alpha)$.

This is called the ***primal problem***.

Consider also the problem of finding $\displaystyle \max_{\alpha:\, \alpha_i \ge 0\ \forall i} \ \min_{x} L(x, \alpha)$.

This is called the ***dual problem***.

It turns out that $\displaystyle \min_{x} \ \max_{\alpha:\, \alpha_i \ge 0\ \forall i} L(x, \alpha) = \max_{\alpha:\, \alpha_i \ge 0\ \forall i} \ \min_{x} L(x, \alpha)$ if a condition called Slater's

condition holds. Slater's condition requires that there is an $x \in \mathbb{R}^{p+1}$ such that $g_i(x) < 0$ for $i = 1, \dots, N$.

The equality $\displaystyle \min_{x} \ \max_{\alpha:\, \alpha_i \ge 0\ \forall i} L(x, \alpha) = \max_{\alpha:\, \alpha_i \ge 0\ \forall i} \ \min_{x} L(x, \alpha)$ is called ***strong duality***.

SOLVING THE DUAL PROBLEM

It also turns out that a solution to our original convex optimization problem is given by a solution to the

primal problem. By strong duality, $\displaystyle \min_{x} \ \max_{\alpha:\, \alpha_i \ge 0\ \forall i} L(x, \alpha) = \max_{\alpha:\, \alpha_i \ge 0\ \forall i} \ \min_{x} L(x, \alpha)$.

So we can find a solution to our convex optimization problem by solving the dual problem. That is, we

want to find $\displaystyle \max_{\alpha:\, \alpha_i \ge 0\ \forall i} \ \min_{x} L(x, \alpha)$. We start by minimizing $L(x, \alpha)$.

To minimize $L(x, \alpha)$, set $\nabla_x L(x, \alpha) = 0$.

$$L(x, \alpha) = \frac{1}{2}||\beta||^2 + \sum_{i=1}^{N} \alpha_i g_i(x)$$

$$= \frac{1}{2}||\beta||^2 + \sum_{i=1}^{N} \alpha_i(1 - y_i(\beta_0 + \cdots + \beta_p x_{ip}))$$

$$= \frac{1}{2}||\beta||^2 - \sum_{i=1}^{N} \alpha_i(y_i(\beta_0 + \cdots + \beta_p x_{ip}) - 1)$$

So $\frac{\partial L}{\partial \beta_j} = \beta_j - \sum_{i=1}^{N} \alpha_i(y_i x_{ij})$ for $j = 1, \dots, N$, and

$$\frac{\partial L}{\partial \beta_0} = -\sum_{i=1}^{N} \alpha_i y_i$$

Setting $\frac{\partial L}{\partial \beta_j} = 0 \implies \beta_j = \sum_{i=1}^{N} \alpha_i y_i x_{ij}$

$$\implies \begin{bmatrix} \beta_1 \\ \vdots \\ \beta_p \end{bmatrix} = \sum_{i=1}^{N} \alpha_i y_i x_i$$

Setting $\frac{\partial L}{\partial \beta_0} = 0 \implies \sum_{i=1}^{N} \alpha_i y_i = 0$

Substituting these values for β into $L(x, \alpha)$, we get

$$L_D(x, \alpha) = \sum_{i=1}^{N} \alpha_i - \frac{1}{2} \sum_{i=1}^{N} \sum_{j=1}^{N} \alpha_i \alpha_j y_i y_j x_i^T x_j. \textbf{(\textit{dual Lagrangian})}$$

Now, we want to find $\underset{\alpha: \alpha_i \geq 0 \ \forall i}{max} L_D(x, \alpha)$.

Our problem now is to $\underset{\alpha}{maximize} \left[\sum_{i=1}^{N} \alpha_i - \frac{1}{2} \sum_{i=1}^{N} \sum_{j=1}^{N} \alpha_i \alpha_j y_i y_j x_i^T x_j \right]$ given the constraints $\alpha_i \geq 0 \ \forall i$ and $\sum_{i=1}^{N} \alpha_i y_i = 0$.

THE COEFFICIENTS FOR THE MAXIMAL MARGIN HYPERPLANE

Once this new convex optimization problem is solved for α, we can find β from $\beta = \sum_{i=1}^{N} \alpha_i y_i x_i$. We can find β_0 from the complementary slackness condition

$\alpha_i g_i(x) = 0 \ \forall i$ given by $\alpha_i \left(1 - y_i(\beta_0 + \cdots + \beta_p x_{ip}) \right) = 0 \ \forall i$.

THE SUPPORT VECTORS

Note that if $\alpha_i > 0$, then $1 - y_i(\beta_0 + \cdots + \beta_p x_{ip}) = 0$.

$$\Rightarrow \quad y_i(\beta_0 + \cdots + \beta_p x_{ip}) = 1 \text{ and } x_i \text{ is called a } \textbf{support vector}.$$

If $y_i(\beta_0 + \cdots + \beta_p x_{ip}) > 1$, then $\alpha_i = 0$ and x_i is not relevant in $\beta = \sum_{i=1}^{N} \alpha_i y_i x_i$. β is a linear combination of only the support vectors.

CLASSIFYING TEST POINTS

If we let $\hat{f}(x) = \beta_0^* + \beta_1^* x_1 + \cdots + \beta_p^* x_p$, where $x = (x_1, \ldots, x_p)$ is arbitrary in $\mathbb{R}^p$ and $(\beta_0^*, \beta_1^*, \ldots, \beta_p^*)$ is the solution to our optimization problem, note that we can rewrite $\hat{f}(x)$ as $x^T \beta^* + \beta_0^*$, or equivalently $\langle x, \beta^* \rangle + \beta_0^*$ where $\langle x, \beta^* \rangle$ is the dot product between x and β^*. It's also called the inner product, although an inner product is more general than the dot product.

Since $\beta^* = \sum_{i=1}^{N} \alpha_i y_i x_i$, we have that $\langle x, \beta^* \rangle + \beta_0^* = \langle x, \sum_{i=1}^{N} \alpha_i y_i x_i \rangle + \beta_0^*$

$$= \sum_{i=1}^{N} \alpha_i y_i \langle x, x_i \rangle + \beta_0^*$$

So we can write $\hat{f}(x) = \sum_{i=1}^{N} \alpha_i y_i \langle x, x_i \rangle + \beta_0^*$, and any test point x is classified according to the sign of $\hat{f}(x)$.

MAXIMAL MARGIN CLASSIFIER EXAMPLE 1

Suppose we have the following data points:

$x_1 = (1, 3), x_2 = (2, 1), x_3 = (3, 2)$ with $y_1 = -1, y_2 = 1, y_3 = 1$.

Find the maximal margin hyperplane and identify any support vectors.

Solution:

Our convex optimization problem takes the form:

$\underset{(\beta_0, \beta) \in \mathbb{R}^3}{minimize} f(\beta_0, \beta_1, \beta_2)$ given the constraint

$$g_i(\beta_0, \beta_1, \beta_2) \le 0 \text{ for } i = 1, 2, 3, \text{ where}$$

$$f(\beta_0, \beta_1, \beta_2) = \frac{1}{2}||\beta||^2 \text{ and}$$

$$g_i(\beta_0, \beta_1, \beta_2) = 1 - y_i(\beta_0 + \beta_1 x_{i1} + \beta_2 x_{i2}) \text{ for } i = 1, 2, 3.$$

So $g_1 = 1 + (\beta_0 + \beta_1 + 3\beta_2)$

$g_2 = 1 - (\beta_0 + 2\beta_1 + \beta_2)$

$g_3 = 1 - (\beta_0 + 3\beta_1 + 2\beta_2).$

The dual Lagrangian is given by

$$L_D(x, \alpha) = \sum_{i=1}^{3} \alpha_i - \frac{1}{2} \sum_{i=1}^{3} \sum_{j=1}^{3} \alpha_i \alpha_j y_i y_j x_i^T x_j$$

So $L_D(x, \alpha) = (\alpha_1 + \alpha_2 + \alpha_3) - \frac{1}{2}[10\alpha_1^2 + 5\alpha_2^2 + 13\alpha_3^2 - 10\alpha_1\alpha_2 - 18\alpha_1\alpha_3 + 16\alpha_2\alpha_3]$

We want to maximize $L_D(x, \alpha)$ subject to the constraints $\alpha_i \ge 0 \ \forall i$ and $\alpha_1 y_1 + \alpha_2 y_2 + \alpha_3 y_3 = 0$.

That is, we need $\alpha_i \ge 0 \ \forall i$ and $-\alpha_1 + \alpha_2 + \alpha_3 = 0$.

Using $\alpha_1 = \alpha_2 + \alpha_3$, rewrite L_D as follows:

$$L_D = 2(\alpha_2 + \alpha_3) - \frac{1}{2}[10(\alpha_2 + \alpha_3)^2 + 5\alpha_2^2 + 13\alpha_3^2 - 10(\alpha_2 + \alpha_3)\alpha_2 - 18(\alpha_2 + \alpha_3)\alpha_3 + 16\alpha_2\alpha_3]$$

Simplifying, we get $L_D = 2(\alpha_2 + \alpha_3) - \frac{1}{2}[5\alpha_2^2 + 8\alpha_2\alpha_3 + 5\alpha_3^2].$

So we want to maximize L_D subject to the constraints $\alpha_2 \ge 0$ and $\alpha_3 \ge 0$.

So we're maximizing L_D on the positive orthant $\alpha_2 \ge 0, \alpha_3 \ge 0$.

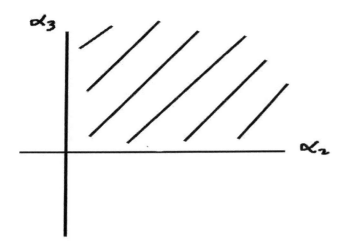

Let's look for any critical points in the interior of the positive orthant by setting $\nabla L_D = 0$.

$$\frac{\partial L_D}{\partial \alpha_2} = 2 - 5\alpha_2 - 4\alpha_3$$

$$\frac{\partial L_D}{\partial \alpha_3} = 2 - 4\alpha_2 - 5\alpha_3$$

Setting $\nabla L_D = 0 \quad \Longrightarrow \quad -5\alpha_2 - 4\alpha_3 = -2$

$$-4\alpha_2 - 5\alpha_3 = -2$$

$$\Longrightarrow \quad \alpha_2 = \frac{2}{9} \text{ and } \alpha_3 = \frac{2}{9}.$$

So $\left(\frac{2}{9}, \frac{2}{9}\right)$ is a critical point in the interior of the positive orthant.

$$L_D\big|_{\left(\frac{2}{9},\frac{2}{9}\right)} = \frac{4}{9}$$

Using the second derivative test, we can show that $L_D(\alpha)$ has a local max at $\left(\frac{2}{9}, \frac{2}{9}\right)$. However, a local max of a concave function on a convex set is a global max. $L_D(\alpha_2, \alpha_3)$ is a concave function and the positive orthant $E = \{(\alpha_2, \alpha_3) | \alpha_2, \alpha_3 \geq 0\}$ is convex. (Note $L_D(\alpha_1, \alpha_2, \alpha_3)$ is also concave.) Hence, $L_D(\alpha_2, \alpha_3)$ has a global max on E.

$L_D(\alpha_1, \alpha_2, \alpha_3)$ has a global max at $(\alpha_1, \alpha_2, \alpha_3)$ over the set $F = \{(\alpha_1, \alpha_2, \alpha_3) | \alpha_1 = \alpha_2 + \alpha_3, \alpha_2 \geq 0, \alpha_3 \geq 0\}$ if and only if $L_D(\alpha_2, \alpha_3)$ has a global max at (α_2, α_3) over the set E.

It follows that $L_D(\alpha_1, \alpha_2, \alpha_3)$ has a global max at $\left(\frac{4}{9}, \frac{2}{9}, \frac{2}{9}\right)$.

$$\alpha_2 = \frac{2}{9}$$

$$\alpha_3 = \frac{2}{9}$$

$$\implies \alpha_1 = \frac{4}{9}.$$

$$\beta = \sum_{i=1}^{3} \alpha_i y_i x_i = -\frac{4}{9}\begin{bmatrix} 1 \\ 3 \end{bmatrix} + \frac{2}{9}\begin{bmatrix} 2 \\ 1 \end{bmatrix} + \frac{2}{9}\begin{bmatrix} 3 \\ 2 \end{bmatrix} = \begin{bmatrix} 6/9 \\ -6/9 \end{bmatrix} = \begin{bmatrix} 2/3 \\ -2/3 \end{bmatrix}$$

$$\implies \beta_1 = \frac{2}{3}, \beta_2 = -\frac{2}{3}.$$

By complementary slackness, $\alpha_i(1 - y_i(\beta_0 + \beta_1 x_{i1} + \beta_2 x_{i2})) = 0 \; \forall i.$

For $i = 1$, we get $\frac{4}{9}\left(1 + (\beta_0 + \frac{2}{3}\cdot 1 - \frac{2}{3}\cdot 3)\right) = 0$

$$\implies \qquad 1 + \beta_0 + \frac{2}{3} - 2 = 0$$

$$\implies \qquad \beta_0 = \frac{1}{3}$$

$$\implies \qquad \beta_0 = \frac{1}{3}$$

$$\beta_1 = \frac{2}{3}$$

$$\beta_2 = -\frac{2}{3}$$

$\implies \qquad$ Our hyperplane is given by $\beta_0 + \beta_1 X_1 + \beta_2 X_2 = 0.$

$\qquad$ So we have $\frac{1}{3} + \frac{2}{3}X_1 - \frac{2}{3}X_2 = 0$

$$\implies \qquad 1 + 2X_1 - 2X_2 = 0$$

$$\implies \qquad X_2 = X_1 + \frac{1}{2}.$$

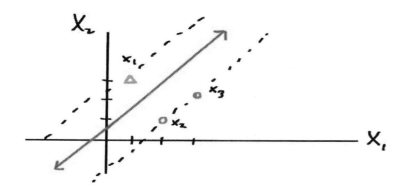

Since $\alpha_1, \alpha_2,$ and α_3 are all nonzero, we have that each x_i satisfies $y_i(\beta_0 + \beta_1 x_{i1} + \beta_2 x_{i2}) = 1$. Hence, $x_1, x_2,$ and x_3 all lie on the margin and are, therefore, support vectors.

MAXIMAL MARGIN CLASSIFIER EXAMPLE 2

Suppose we have the following data points:

$x_1 = (1, 3), x_2 = (2, 1), x_3 = (3, -1)$ with $y_1 = -1, y_2 = 1, y_3 = 1$.

Find the maximal margin hyperplane and identify any support vectors.

Solution:

Our convex optimization problem takes the form:

$\underset{(\beta_0, \beta) \in \mathbb{R}^3}{minimize} f(\beta_0, \beta_1, \beta_2)$ given the constraint

$$g_i(\beta_0, \beta_1, \beta_2) \leq 0 \text{ for } i = 1, 2, 3, \text{ where}$$

$$f(\beta_0, \beta_1, \beta_2) = \frac{1}{2}||\beta||^2 \text{ and}$$

$$g_i(\beta_0, \beta_1, \beta_2) = 1 - y_i(\beta_0 + \beta_1 x_{i1} + \beta_2 x_{i2}) \text{ for } i = 1, 2, 3.$$

So $\quad g_1 = 1 + (\beta_0 + \beta_1 + 3\beta_2)$

$g_2 = 1 - (\beta_0 + 2\beta_1 + \beta_2)$

$g_3 = 1 - (\beta_0 + 3\beta_1 - \beta_2)$.

The dual Lagrangian is given by

$$L_D(x, \alpha) = \sum_{i=1}^{3} \alpha_i - \frac{1}{2}\sum_{i=1}^{3}\sum_{j=1}^{3} \alpha_i \alpha_j y_i y_j x_i^T x_j$$

So $L_D(x, \alpha) = (\alpha_1 + \alpha_2 + \alpha_3) - \frac{1}{2}[10\alpha_1^2 + 5\alpha_2^2 + 10\alpha_3^2 - 10\alpha_1\alpha_2 + 10\alpha_2\alpha_3]$

We want to maximize $L_D(x, \alpha)$ subject to the constraints $\alpha_i \geq 0 \ \forall i$ and $\alpha_1 y_1 + \alpha_2 y_2 + \alpha_3 y_3 = 0$.

That is, we need $\alpha_i \geq 0 \ \forall i$ and $-\alpha_1 + \alpha_2 + \alpha_3 = 0$.

Using $\alpha_1 = \alpha_2 + \alpha_3$, rewrite L_D as follows:

$$L_D = 2(\alpha_2 + \alpha_3) - \frac{1}{2}[10(\alpha_2 + \alpha_3)^2 + 5\alpha_2^2 + 10\alpha_3^2 - 10(\alpha_2 + \alpha_3)\alpha_2 + 10\alpha_2\alpha_3]$$

Simplifying, we get $L_D = 2(\alpha_2 + \alpha_3) - \frac{1}{2}[5(\alpha_2 + 2\alpha_3)^2]$.

$$= 2(\alpha_2 + \alpha_3) - \frac{5}{2}(\alpha_2 + 2\alpha_3)^2$$

So we want to maximize L_D subject to the constraints $\alpha_2 \geq 0$ and $\alpha_3 \geq 0$.

So we're maximizing L_D on the positive orthant $\alpha_2 \geq 0, \alpha_3 \geq 0$.

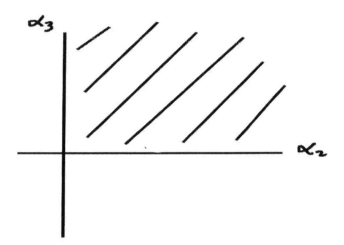

Let's look for any critical points in the interior of the positive orthant by setting $\nabla L_D = 0$.

$$\frac{\partial L_D}{\partial \alpha_2} = 2 - 5(\alpha_2 + 2\alpha_3)$$

$$\frac{\partial L_D}{\partial \alpha_3} = 2 - 5(\alpha_2 + 2\alpha_3) \cdot 2$$

Setting $\nabla L_D = 0$ $\implies$ $5(\alpha_2 + 2\alpha_3) = 2$

$$10(\alpha_2 + 2\alpha_3) = 2$$

$\implies$ contradiction

There is no critical point in the interior of $\{(\alpha_2, \alpha_3) | \alpha_2, \alpha_3 \geq 0\}$.

We need to check the boundaries $\alpha_2 = 0$ and $\alpha_3 = 0$.

On $\alpha_2 = 0$, L_D has a local max at $\alpha_3 = \frac{1}{10}$ relative to the boundary $\alpha_2 = 0, \alpha_3 \geq 0$. The value of L_D at $(\alpha_2, \alpha_3) = \left(0, \frac{1}{10}\right)$ is $\frac{1}{10}$.

On $\alpha_3 = 0$, L_D has a local max at $\alpha_2 = \frac{2}{5}$ relative to the boundary $\alpha_3 = 0, \alpha_2 \geq 0$. The value of L_D at $(\alpha_2, \alpha_3) = \left(\frac{2}{5}, 0\right)$ is $\frac{2}{5} > \frac{1}{10}$.

Since every global max is a local max, the global max has to occur at a critical point relative to a portion of the boundary. Since the local max at $\left(\frac{2}{5}, 0\right)$ is greater than the local max at $\left(0, \frac{1}{10}\right)$, the candidate for the global max is $\left(\frac{2}{5}, 0\right)$. In fact, we can show that, for a fixed α_3, the local max value relative to the line $l_{\alpha_3} = \{(\alpha_2, \alpha_3) | \alpha_2 \geq 0\}$ decreases as α_3 increases. Therefore, there is a global max at $\left(\frac{2}{5}, 0\right)$.

$L_D(\alpha_2, \alpha_3)$ has a global max at (α_2, α_3) over the positive orthant $\{(\alpha_2, \alpha_3) | \alpha_2, \alpha_3 \geq 0\}$ if and only if $L_D(\alpha_1, \alpha_2, \alpha_3)$ has a global max at $(\alpha_1, \alpha_2, \alpha_3)$ over the set $\{(\alpha_1, \alpha_2, \alpha_3) | \alpha_1 = \alpha_2 + \alpha_3, \alpha_2 \geq 0, \alpha_3 \geq 0\}$.

It follows that $L_D(\alpha_1, \alpha_2, \alpha_3)$ has a global max at $\left(\frac{2}{5}, \frac{2}{5}, 0\right)$.

$$\alpha_2 = \frac{2}{5}$$

$$\alpha_3 = 0$$

$$\Rightarrow \alpha_1 = \frac{2}{5}.$$

$$\beta = \sum_{i=1}^{3} \alpha_i y_i x_i = -\frac{2}{5}\begin{bmatrix} 1 \\ 3 \end{bmatrix} + \frac{2}{5}\begin{bmatrix} 2 \\ 1 \end{bmatrix} = \begin{bmatrix} 2/5 \\ -4/5 \end{bmatrix}$$

$$\Rightarrow \beta_1 = \frac{2}{5}, \beta_2 = -\frac{4}{5}.$$

By complementary slackness, $\alpha_i (1 - y_i(\beta_0 + \beta_1 x_{i1} + \beta_2 x_{i2})) = 0 \; \forall i.$

For $i = 1$, we get $\frac{2}{5}\left(1 + (\beta_0 + \frac{2}{5} - \frac{4}{5} \cdot 3)\right) = 0$

$$\Rightarrow \qquad 1 + \beta_0 + \frac{2}{5} - \frac{12}{5} = 0$$

$$\Rightarrow \qquad \beta_0 = 1$$

$$\Rightarrow \qquad \beta_0 = 1$$

$$\beta_1 = \frac{2}{5}$$

$$\beta_2 = -\frac{4}{5}$$

$$\Rightarrow \qquad \text{Our hyperplane is given by } \beta_0 + \beta_1 X_1 + \beta_2 X_2 = 0.$$

$$\text{So we have } 1 + \frac{2}{5}X_1 - \frac{4}{5}X_2 = 0$$

$$\Rightarrow \qquad 5 + 2X_1 - 4X_2 = 0$$

$$\Rightarrow \qquad 4X_2 = 2X_1 + 5$$

$$\Rightarrow \qquad X_2 = \tfrac{1}{2}X_1 + \tfrac{5}{4}$$

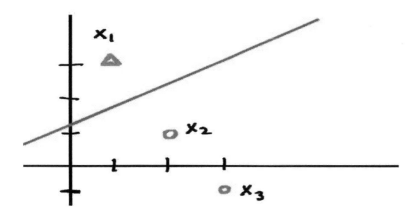

Since α_1 and α_2 are nonzero, we have that x_1 and x_2 satisfy $y_i(\beta_0 + \beta_1 x_{i1} + \beta_2 x_{i2}) = 1$. Hence, x_1 and x_2 lie on the margin and are, therefore, support vectors.

SUMMARY: MAXIMAL MARGIN CLASSIFIER

- If the $x_i's$ of our data are separable by a hyperplane, we want to find the separating hyperplane that has maximal margin.

- Once we find the maximal margin hyperplane, we can classify new points depending on which side of the hyperplane the new point lies on.

- In trying to find the maximal margin hyperplane, we end up with a convex optimization problem, which is solved using Lagrange multipliers.

PROBLEM SET: MAXIMAL MARGIN CLASSIFIER

1. Suppose we have the following data points:

   $x_1 = (1,1), x_2 = (2,3), x_3 = (3,1)$ with $y_1 = 1, y_2 = -1, y_3 = -1$.

   Find the maximal margin hyperplane and identify any support vectors.

2. Suppose we have the following data points:

   $x_1 = (1,1), x_2 = (2,3), x_3 = (3,1), x_4 = (0,2)$ with $y_1 = 1, y_2 = -1, y_3 = -1, y_4 = 1$.

   Find the maximal margin hyperplane and identify any support vectors.

SOLUTION SET: MAXIMAL MARGIN CLASSIFIER

1. Our convex optimization problem takes the form:

$$\underset{(\beta_0,\beta)\in\mathbb{R}^3}{\text{minimize}} \quad f(\beta_0,\beta_1,\beta_2) \qquad \text{given the constraint } g_i(\beta_0,\beta_1,\beta_2) \leq 0 \text{ for } i = 1,2,3$$

$$\text{where } f(\beta_0,\beta_1,\beta_2) = \frac{1}{2}\|\beta\|^2$$

$$\text{and } g_i(\beta_0,\beta_1,\beta_2) = 1 - y_i(\beta_0 + \beta_1 x_{i1} + \beta_2 x_{i2}) \text{ for } i = 1,2,3$$

So $\quad g_1 = 1 - (\beta_0 + \beta_1 + \beta_2)$

$\quad g_2 = 1 + (\beta_0 + 2\beta_1 + 3\beta_2)$

$\quad g_3 = 1 + (\beta_0 + 3\beta_1 + \beta_2)$

The dual Lagrangian is given by $L_D(x,\alpha) = \sum_{i=1}^{3} \alpha_i - \frac{1}{2}\sum_{i=1}^{3}\sum_{j=1}^{3} \alpha_i\alpha_j y_i y_j x_i^T x_j.$

So $L_D(x,\alpha) = (\alpha_1 + \alpha_2 + \alpha_3) - \frac{1}{2}[2\alpha_1^2 + 13\alpha_2^2 + 10\alpha_3^2 - 10\alpha_1\alpha_2 - 8\alpha_1\alpha_3 + 18\alpha_2\alpha_3]$

We want to maximize $L_D(x,\alpha)$ subject to the constraints $\alpha_i \geq 0 \, \forall \, i$ and $\alpha_1 y_1 + \alpha_2 y_2 + \alpha_3 y_3 = 0$. That is, we need $\alpha_i \geq 0 \, \forall \, i$ and $\alpha_1 - \alpha_2 - \alpha_3 = 0$. Using $\alpha_1 = \alpha_2 + \alpha_3$, rewrite L_D as follows:

$$L_D = 2(\alpha_2 + \alpha_3) - \frac{1}{2}[2(\alpha_2 + \alpha_3)^2 + 13\alpha_2^2 + 10\alpha_3^2 - 10(\alpha_2 + \alpha_3)\alpha_2 - 8(\alpha_2 + \alpha_3)\alpha_3 + 18\alpha_2\alpha_3]$$

Simplifying, we get

$$L_D = 2(\alpha_2 + \alpha_3) - \frac{1}{2}[5\alpha_2^2 + 4\alpha_2\alpha_3 + 4\alpha_3^2]$$

So we want to maximize L_D subject to the constraints $\alpha_2 \geq 0$ and $\alpha_3 \geq 0$.

So we're maximizing L_D on the positive orthant $\alpha_2 \geq 0, \alpha_3 \geq 0$:

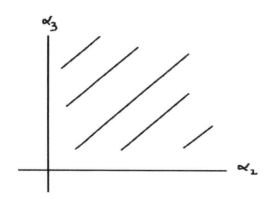

Let's look for any critical points in the interior of the positive orthant by setting $\nabla L_D = 0$.

$$\frac{\partial L_D}{\partial \alpha_2} = 2 - \frac{1}{2}(10\alpha_2 + 4\alpha_3) = 2 - (5\alpha_2 + 2\alpha_3)$$

$$\frac{\partial L_D}{\partial \alpha_3} = 2 - \frac{1}{2}(4\alpha_2 + 8\alpha_3) = 2 - (2\alpha_2 + 4\alpha_3)$$

Setting $\nabla L_D = 0 \Rightarrow 5\alpha_2 + 2\alpha_3 = 2$

$$2\alpha_2 + 4\alpha_3 = 2$$

$$\Rightarrow \alpha_2 = \frac{1}{4} \text{ and } \alpha_3 = \frac{3}{8}$$

So $\left(\frac{1}{4}, \frac{3}{8}\right)$ is a critical point in the interior of the positive orthant.

$$L_D\big|_{\left(\frac{1}{4}, \frac{3}{8}\right)} = \frac{5}{8}.$$

Using the second derivative test, we can show that $L_D(\alpha)$ has a local max at $\left(\frac{1}{4}, \frac{3}{8}\right)$. However, a local max of a concave function on a convex set is a global max. $L_D(\alpha_2, \alpha_3)$ is a concave function and the positive orthant $E = \{(\alpha_2, \alpha_3) | \alpha_2, \alpha_3 \geq 0\}$ is convex. Hence, $L_D(\alpha_2, \alpha_3)$ has a global max on E. $L_D(\alpha_1, \alpha_2, \alpha_3)$ has a global max at $(\alpha_1, \alpha_2, \alpha_3)$ over the set

$$F = \{(\alpha_1, \alpha_2, \alpha_3) | \alpha_1 = \alpha_2 + \alpha_3, \alpha_2 \geq 0, \alpha_3 \geq 0\}$$

if and only if $L_D(\alpha_2, \alpha_3)$ has a global max at (α_2, α_3) over the set E. It follows that $L_D(\alpha_1, \alpha_2, \alpha_3)$ has a global max at $\left(\frac{5}{8}, \frac{1}{4}, \frac{3}{8}\right)$. $\left(\alpha_1 = \alpha_2 + \alpha_3 = \frac{1}{4} + \frac{3}{8} = \frac{5}{8}\right)$

$$\beta = \sum_{i=1}^{3} \alpha_i y_i x_i = \frac{5}{8}\begin{bmatrix}1\\1\end{bmatrix} - \frac{1}{4}\begin{bmatrix}2\\3\end{bmatrix} - \frac{3}{8}\begin{bmatrix}3\\1\end{bmatrix} = \begin{bmatrix}-1\\-\frac{1}{2}\end{bmatrix}$$

$$\Rightarrow \beta_1 = -1, \beta_2 = -\frac{1}{2}.$$

By complementary slackness, $\alpha_i\left(1 - y_i(\beta_0 + \beta_1 x_{i1} + \beta_2 x_{i2})\right) = 0 \,\forall\, i$

For $i = 1$, we get $\frac{5}{8}\left(1 - (\beta_0 + \beta_1 + \beta_2)\right) = 0$

$$\Rightarrow 1 - \left(\beta_0 + (-1) - \frac{1}{2}\right) = 0$$

$$\Rightarrow \beta_0 = \frac{5}{2}.$$

$$\Rightarrow \beta_0 = \frac{5}{2}$$

$$\beta_1 = -1$$

$$\beta_2 = -\frac{1}{2}$$

Our hyperplane is given by $\beta_0 + \beta_1 X_1 + \beta_2 X_2 = 0$.

So we have $\frac{5}{2} - X_1 - \frac{1}{2}X_2 = 0$

$$\Rightarrow \quad X_2 = -2X_1 + 5$$

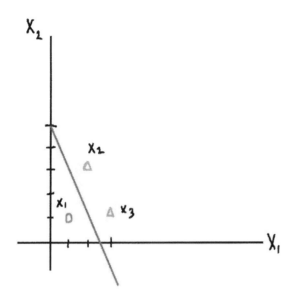

Since $\alpha_1, \alpha_2, \alpha_3$ are all nonzero, we have that each x_i satisfies $y_i(\beta_0 + \beta_1 x_{i1} + \beta_2 x_{i2}) = 1$. Hence, x_1, x_2, x_3 all lie on the margin and are, therefore, support vectors.

2. Our convex optimization problem takes the form:

$$\underset{(\beta_0, \beta) \in \mathbb{R}^3}{\text{minimize}} \quad f(\beta_0, \beta_1, \beta_2) \qquad \text{given the constraint } g_i(\beta_0, \beta_1, \beta_2) \leq 0 \text{ for } i = 1,2,3,4$$

$$\text{where } f(\beta_0, \beta_1, \beta_2) = \frac{1}{2}\|\beta\|^2 \text{ and}$$

$$g_i(\beta_0, \beta_1, \beta_2) = 1 - y_i(\beta_0 + \beta_1 x_{i1} + \beta_2 x_{i2}) \text{ for } i = 1,2,3,4$$

So $\quad g_1 = 1 - (\beta_0 + \beta_1 + \beta_2)$
$\quad g_2 = 1 + (\beta_0 + 2\beta_1 + 3\beta_2)$
$\quad g_3 = 1 + (\beta_0 + 3\beta_1 + \beta_2)$
$\quad g_4 = 1 - (\beta_0 + 2\beta_2)$

The dual Lagrangian is given by $L_D(x, \alpha) = \sum_{i=1}^{4} \alpha_i - \frac{1}{2}\sum_{i=1}^{4}\sum_{j=1}^{4} \alpha_i \alpha_j y_i y_j x_i^T x_j$.

So $L_D(x, \alpha) = (\alpha_1 + \alpha_2 + \alpha_3 + \alpha_4) - \frac{1}{2}[2\alpha_1^2 + 13\alpha_2^2 + 10\alpha_3^2 + 4\alpha_4^2 - 10\alpha_1\alpha_2 - 8\alpha_1\alpha_3 + 4\alpha_1\alpha_4 + 18\alpha_2\alpha_3 - 12\alpha_2\alpha_4 - 4\alpha_3\alpha_4]$

We want to maximize $L_D(x, \alpha)$ subject to the constraints $\alpha_i \geq 0 \ \forall \ i$ and $\alpha_1 y_1 + \alpha_2 y_2 + \alpha_3 y_3 + \alpha_4 y_4 = 0$. That is, we need $\alpha_i \geq 0 \ \forall \ i$ and $\alpha_1 - \alpha_2 - \alpha_3 + \alpha_4 = 0$. Using $\alpha_1 = \alpha_2 + \alpha_3 - \alpha_4$, rewrite L_D as follows:

$$L_D = 2(\alpha_2 + \alpha_3) - \frac{1}{2}[2(\alpha_2 + \alpha_3 - \alpha_4)^2 + 13\alpha_2^2 + 10\alpha_3^2 + 4\alpha_4^2 - 10(\alpha_2 + \alpha_3 - \alpha_4)\alpha_2 - 8(\alpha_2 + \alpha_3 - \alpha_4)\alpha_3 + 4(\alpha_2 + \alpha_3 - \alpha_4)\alpha_4 + 18\alpha_2\alpha_3 - 12\alpha_2\alpha_4 - 4\alpha_3\alpha_4]$$

Simplifying, we get

$$L_D = 2(\alpha_2 + \alpha_3) - \frac{1}{2}[5\alpha_2^2 + 4\alpha_3^2 + 2\alpha_4^2 + 4\alpha_2\alpha_3 - 2\alpha_2\alpha_4 + 4\alpha_3\alpha_4]$$

So we want to maximize L_D subject to the constraints $\alpha_2, \alpha_3, \alpha_4 \geq 0$.

So we're maximizing L_D on the positive orthant $\alpha_2, \alpha_3, \alpha_4 \geq 0$.

Let's look for any critical points in the interior of the positive orthant by setting $\nabla L_D = 0$.

$$\frac{\partial L_D}{\partial \alpha_2} = 2 - 5\alpha_2 - 2\alpha_3 - \alpha_4$$

$$\frac{\partial L_D}{\partial \alpha_3} = 2 - 4\alpha_3 - 2\alpha_2 - 2\alpha_4$$

$$\frac{\partial L_D}{\partial \alpha_4} = -2\alpha_4 + \alpha_2 - 2\alpha_3$$

Setting $\nabla L_D = 0 \Longrightarrow -5\alpha_2 - 2\alpha_3 - \alpha_4 = -2$

$$-2\alpha_2 - 4\alpha_3 - 2\alpha_4 = -2$$

$$\alpha_2 - 2\alpha_3 - 2\alpha_4 = 0$$

The solution to this system is $\alpha_2 = \frac{1}{4}, \alpha_3 = \frac{5}{8}, \alpha_4 = -\frac{1}{2}$. However, since α_4 is negative, this solution is not in the interior of the positive orthant.

We need to check the boundaries $\alpha_2 = 0, \alpha_3 = 0$, and $\alpha_4 = 0$.

On $\alpha_2 = 0$, there are no critical points in the interior of the face $\alpha_2 = 0$.

On $\alpha_3 = 0$, L_D has a local max at $(\alpha_2, \alpha_4) = \left(\frac{4}{9}, \frac{2}{9}\right)$ relative to the boundary $\alpha_3 = 0, \alpha_2 \geq 0, \alpha_4 \geq 0$.

The value of L_D at $(\alpha_2, \alpha_4) = \left(\frac{4}{9}, \frac{2}{9}\right)$ is $\frac{4}{9}$.

On $\alpha_4 = 0$, L_D has a local max at $(\alpha_2, \alpha_3) = \left(\frac{1}{4}, \frac{3}{8}\right)$ relative to the boundary $\alpha_4 = 0, \alpha_2, \alpha_3 \geq 0$. The value of L_D at $(\alpha_2, \alpha_3) = \left(\frac{1}{4}, \frac{3}{8}\right)$ is $\frac{5}{8}$.

Since $\frac{5}{8} > \frac{4}{9}$, the candidate for the global max is $\left(\frac{1}{4}, \frac{3}{8}, 0\right)$. In fact, we can show that, for a fixed α_4, the local max value relative to the plane $l_{\alpha_4} = \{(\alpha_2, \alpha_3, \alpha_4) | \alpha_2, \alpha_3 \geq 0\}$ decreases as α_4 increases. (The local max occurs at $(\alpha_2, \alpha_3) = \left(\frac{1}{4}, \frac{3}{8} - \frac{\alpha_4}{2}\right)$ and $L_D = \frac{5}{8} - \frac{1}{2}(\alpha_4^2 + \alpha_4)$ there.)

Therefore, there is a global max at $\left(\frac{1}{4}, \frac{3}{8}, 0\right)$.

$L_D(\alpha_2, \alpha_3, \alpha_4)$ has a global max at $(\alpha_2, \alpha_3, \alpha_4)$ over the positive orthant $\{(\alpha_2, \alpha_3, \alpha_4) | \alpha_2, \alpha_3, \alpha_4 \geq 0\}$ if and only if $L_D(\alpha_1, \alpha_2, \alpha_3, \alpha_4)$ has a global max at $(\alpha_1, \alpha_2, \alpha_3, \alpha_4)$ over the set

$$\{(\alpha_1, \alpha_2, \alpha_3, \alpha_4) | \alpha_1 = \alpha_2 + \alpha_3 - \alpha_4, \alpha_2 \geq 0, \alpha_3 \geq 0, \alpha_4 \geq 0\}.$$

It follows that $L_D(\alpha_1, \alpha_2, \alpha_3, \alpha_4)$ has a global max at $\left(\frac{5}{8}, \frac{1}{4}, \frac{3}{8}, 0\right)$.

$$\left(\alpha_1 = \alpha_2 + \alpha_3 - \alpha_4 = \frac{1}{4} + \frac{3}{8} - 0 = \frac{5}{8}\right)$$

$$\beta = \sum_{i=1}^{4} \alpha_i y_i x_i = \frac{5}{8}\begin{bmatrix} 1 \\ 1 \end{bmatrix} - \frac{1}{4}\begin{bmatrix} 2 \\ 3 \end{bmatrix} - \frac{3}{8}\begin{bmatrix} 3 \\ 1 \end{bmatrix} = \begin{bmatrix} -1 \\ 1 \\ -\frac{1}{2} \end{bmatrix}$$

$$\Longrightarrow \beta_1 = -1, \beta_2 = -\frac{1}{2}.$$

By complementary slackness, $\alpha_i\left(1 - y_i(\beta_0 + \beta_1 x_{i1} + \beta_2 x_{i2})\right) = 0 \; \forall \; i$

For $i = 1$, we get $\frac{5}{8}\left(1 - (\beta_0 + \beta_1 + \beta_2)\right) = 0$

$$\Longrightarrow 1 - \left(\beta_0 + (-1) - \frac{1}{2}\right) = 0$$

$$\Longrightarrow \beta_0 = \frac{5}{2}.$$

$$\Longrightarrow \beta_0 = \frac{5}{2}$$

$$\beta_1 = -1$$

$$\beta_2 = -\frac{1}{2}$$

Our hyperplane is given by $\beta_0 + \beta_1 X_1 + \beta_2 X_2 = 0$.

So we have $\frac{5}{2} - X_1 - \frac{1}{2}X_2 = 0$

$$\Longrightarrow X_2 = -2X_1 + 5$$

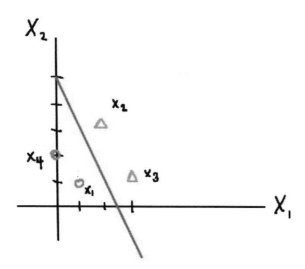

Since $\alpha_1, \alpha_2, \alpha_3$ are all nonzero, we have that x_1, x_2, x_3 satisfy $y_i(\beta_0 + \beta_1 x_{i1} + \beta_2 x_{i2}) = 1$. Hence, x_1, x_2, x_3 lie on the margin and are, therefore, support vectors. Notice that our hyperplane is exactly the same line we got for problem 1.

7 – SUPPORT VECTOR CLASSIFIER

SUPPORT VECTOR CLASSIFIER

We have seen how the maximal margin hyperplane can be found when the x_i's are separable by a hyperplane. If the x_i's are not separable by a hyperplane, we can still try to find a hyperplane that separates most of the points but that may have some points that lie inside the margin or lie on the wrong side of the hyperplane. Here's what such a scenario might look like:

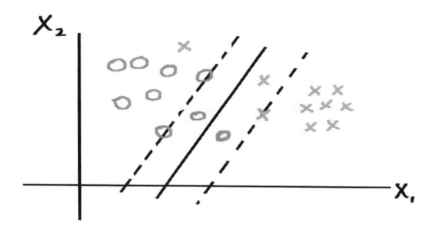

The method we will look at is called the ***support vector classifier***, also called the ***soft margin classifier*** because the margin can be penetrated by points from either side.

Just as in the case of the maximal margin classifier, we want our hyperplane to be as far as possible from each point that's on the correct side of the hyperplane. So points on the margin or outside the margin but on the correct side of the hyperplane will be as far as possible from the hyperplane. Points inside the margin but on the correct side of the hyperplane will be as far as possible from the hyperplane and as close as possible to the margin boundary.

For those points on the wrong side of the hyperplane, we want those points to be as close to the hyperplane as possible.

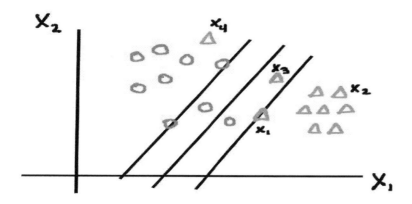

x_1 is on the margin. x_2 is outside the margin but on the correct side of the hyperplane. x_3 is inside the margin but on the correct side. x_4 is on the wrong side of the hyperplane. Let's make all of this more precise.

In the discussion of the maximal margin classifier, we've seen that the perpendicular distance between x_i and the hyperplane $\beta_0 + \beta_1 X_1 + \cdots + \beta_p X_p = 0$ is given by

$$\frac{1}{||\beta||} \begin{cases} \beta_0 + \beta_1 x_{i1} + \cdots + \beta_p x_{ip}, & if\ \beta_0 + \beta_1 x_{i1} + \cdots + \beta_p x_{ip} > 0 \\ -(\beta_0 + \beta_1 x_{i1} + \cdots + \beta_p x_{ip}), & if\ \beta_0 + \beta_1 x_{i1} + \cdots + \beta_p x_{ip} < 0 \end{cases}$$

So the signed perpendicular distance between x_i and the hyperplane is given by

$$\frac{1}{||\beta||} y_i (\beta_0 + \beta_1 x_{i1} + \cdots + \beta_p x_{ip}).$$

This expression is positive if x_i is on the correct side of the hyperplane. It's negative if x_i is on the wrong side of the hyperplane.

SLACK VARIABLES: POINTS ON CORRECT SIDE OF HYPERPLANE

In order to characterize each point x_i, we introduce variables ε_i called ***slack variables*** for each x_i, where $i = 1, \dots, N$.

If x_i is on the correct side of the hyperplane but inside the margin, then x_i protrudes into the margin by a certain fraction of M.

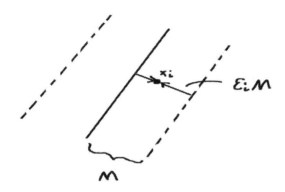

$0 < \varepsilon_i < 1$.

The distance between x_i and the hyperplane is $M - \varepsilon_i M = M(1 - \varepsilon_i)$. However, the distance between x_i and the hyperplane is given by $\frac{1}{||\beta||} y_i \left(\beta_0 + \beta_1 x_{i1} + \cdots + \beta_p x_{ip} \right)$.

So $\frac{1}{||\beta||} y_i \left(\beta_0 + \beta_1 x_{i1} + \cdots + \beta_p x_{ip} \right) = M(1 - \varepsilon_i)$

$\implies \quad \frac{1}{||\beta||} y_i \left(\beta_0 + \beta_1 x_{i1} + \cdots + \beta_p x_{ip} \right) \cdot \frac{1}{1 - \varepsilon_i} = M.$

If x_i is on the correct side of the hyperplane but on or outside the margin, then x_i does not protrude into the margin by any amount.

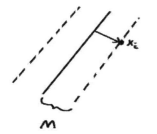 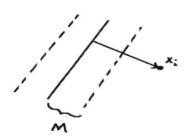

In this case, $\varepsilon_i = 0$. The distance between x_i and the hyperplane is $\frac{1}{||\beta||} y_i (\beta_0 + \beta_1 x_{i1} + \cdots + \beta_p x_{ip})$.
The distance between x_i and the hyperplane is greater than or equal to M.

So $\frac{1}{||\beta||} y_i (\beta_0 + \beta_1 x_{i1} + \cdots + \beta_p x_{ip}) \geq M$.

We can rewrite this as $\frac{1}{||\beta||} y_i (\beta_0 + \beta_1 x_{i1} + \cdots + \beta_p x_{ip}) \cdot \frac{1}{1-\varepsilon_i} \geq M$ since $\varepsilon_i = 0$.

SLACK VARIABLES: POINTS ON WRONG SIDE OF HYPERPLANE

If x_i is on the wrong side of the hyperplane, then x_i protrudes into the margin by a certain multiple of M, $\varepsilon_i M$ where $\varepsilon_i > 1$.

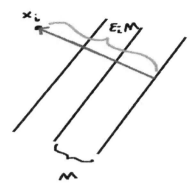

The distance between x_i and the hyperplane is $\varepsilon_i M - M$. The signed distance is therefore $M - \varepsilon_i M$. However, the signed distance between x_i and the hyperplane is given by

$$\frac{1}{||\beta||} y_i (\beta_0 + \beta_1 x_{i1} + \cdots + \beta_p x_{ip}).$$

So $\frac{1}{||\beta||} y_i (\beta_0 + \beta_1 x_{i1} + \cdots + \beta_p x_{ip}) = M - \varepsilon_i M$

$$\implies \quad \frac{1}{||\beta||} y_i (\beta_0 + \beta_1 x_{i1} + \cdots + \beta_p x_{ip}) \cdot \frac{1}{1 - \varepsilon_i} = M$$

FORMULATING THE OPTIMIZATION PROBLEM

Just as in the case of the maximal margin classifier, we want to maximize the margin so that points on the correct side of the hyperplane are as far as possible from the hyperplane.

Not only do we want to maximize the margin, we also want to minimize the violations of the margin, those x_i such that $\varepsilon_i > 0$. Imagine that $\sum_{i=1}^{N} \varepsilon_i \leq K$, where K is some constant called the **tuning parameter**. Since $\varepsilon_i > 1$ corresponds to points on the wrong side of the hyperplane,

$$\sum_{i:\varepsilon_i > 1} \varepsilon_i \geq \sum_{i:\varepsilon_i > 1} 1 = \# \text{ of points on the wrong side of the hyperplane}$$

$$\implies \quad \# \text{ of points on the wrong side of the hyperplane } \leq \sum_{i:\varepsilon_i > 1} \varepsilon_i \leq \sum_{i=1}^{N} \varepsilon_i \leq K.$$

So the number of points on the wrong side of the hyperplane is bounded by K. The lower the value for K, the less leeway for points to violate the margin.

Recall that, in trying to find the maximal margin hyperplane, we needed to solve the optimization problem

$$\underset{(\beta_0,\beta)\in\mathbb{R}^{p+1}}{minimize} \frac{1}{2}||\beta||^2 \quad \text{given the constraint}$$

$$y_i(\beta_0 + \beta_1 x_{i1} + \cdots + \beta_p x_{ip}) \geq 1 \text{ for } i = 1, \ldots, N$$

In trying to find the soft margin hyperplane, we not only want to maximize the margin, but we also want to minimize the violations of the margin. So we need to solve the optimization problem

$$\underset{(\beta_0,\beta,\varepsilon)\in\mathbb{R}^{p+1+N}}{minimize} \frac{1}{2}||\beta||^2 + C\sum_{i=1}^{N}\varepsilon_i \quad \text{given the constraint}$$

$$y_i(\beta_0 + \beta_1 x_{i1} + \cdots + \beta_p x_{ip}) \geq 1 - \varepsilon_i \; \forall i = 1, \ldots, N$$

$$\varepsilon_i \geq 0 \; \forall i = 1, \ldots, N$$

DEFINITION OF SUPPORT VECTOR CLASSIFIER

Once we find $(\beta_0^*, \ldots, \beta_p^*, \varepsilon_1^*, \ldots, \varepsilon_N^*)$ that minimizes $\frac{1}{2}||\beta||^2 + C\sum_{i=1}^{N}\varepsilon_i$, we can use the hyperplane given by $\beta_0^* + \beta_1^* X_1 + \cdots + \beta_p^* X_p = 0$ to classify a test point $(x_1, \ldots, x_p)$ as follows:

If $\beta_0^* + \beta_1^* x_1 + \cdots + \beta_p^* x_p > 0$, then the test point is assigned to class 1.

If $\beta_0^* + \beta_1^* x_1 + \cdots + \beta_p^* x_p < 0$, then the test point is assigned to class -1.

This way of classifying test points is called the ***support vector classifier*** or ***soft margin classifier***.

A CONVEX OPTIMIZATION PROBLEM

Now, let's return to our minimization problem

$$\underset{(\beta_0,\beta,\varepsilon)\in\mathbb{R}^{p+1+N}}{minimize}\frac{1}{2}||\beta||^2 + C\sum_{i=1}^{N}\varepsilon_i \quad \text{given the constraint}$$

$$y_i(\beta_0 + \beta_1 x_{i1} + \cdots + \beta_p x_{ip}) \geq 1 - \varepsilon_i \ \forall i = 1, \dots, N$$

$$\varepsilon_i \geq 0 \ \forall i = 1, \dots, N$$

This is a convex optimization problem, where

$$f: \mathbb{R}^{p+1+N} \longrightarrow \mathbb{R} \text{ given by } f(\beta_0, \dots, \beta_p, \varepsilon_1, \dots, \varepsilon_N) = \frac{1}{2}||\beta||^2 + C\sum_{i=1}^{N}\varepsilon_i, \text{ and}$$

$$g_i: \mathbb{R}^{p+1+N} \longrightarrow \mathbb{R} \text{ given by } g_i(\beta_0, \dots, \beta_p, \varepsilon_1, \dots, \varepsilon_N) = 1 - \varepsilon_i - y_i(\beta_0 + \cdots + \beta_p x_{ip}),$$

$$\text{for } i = 1, \dots, N, \text{ and}$$

$$h_i: \mathbb{R}^{p+1+N} \longrightarrow \mathbb{R} \text{ given by } h_i(\beta_0, \dots, \beta_p, \varepsilon_1, \dots, \varepsilon_N) = -\varepsilon_i, \text{ for } i = 1, \dots, N$$

are differentiable convex functions.

Our convex optimization problem takes the form

$$\underset{(\beta_0,\beta,\varepsilon)\in\mathbb{R}^{p+1+N}}{minimize} f(\beta_0, \dots, \beta_p, \varepsilon_1, \dots, \varepsilon_N) \quad \text{given the constraint}$$

$$g_i(\beta_0, \dots, \beta_p, \varepsilon_1, \dots, \varepsilon_N) \leq 0 \text{ for } i = 1, \dots, N$$

$$h_i(\beta_0, \dots, \beta_p, \varepsilon_1, \dots, \varepsilon_N) \leq 0 \text{ for } i = 1, \dots, N.$$

SOLVING THE CONVEX OPTIMIZATION PROBLEM (SOFT MARGIN)

We can solve this using Lagrange multipliers. Consider the Lagrangian $L: \mathbb{R}^{p+1+N} \times \mathbb{R}^N \times \mathbb{R}^N \longrightarrow \mathbb{R}$ given by $L(x, \alpha, \mu) = f(x) + \sum_{i=1}^{N}\alpha_i g_i(x) + \sum_{i=1}^{N}\mu_i h_i(x)$.

The α_i and μ_i are called Lagrange multipliers.

$$L(x, \alpha, \mu) = \frac{1}{2}||\beta||^2 + C\sum_{i=1}^{N}\varepsilon_i + \sum_{i=1}^{N}\alpha_i(1 - \varepsilon_i - y_i(\beta_0 + \cdots + \beta_p x_{ip})) + \sum_{i=1}^{N}\mu_i(-\varepsilon_i)$$

$$= \frac{1}{2}||\beta||^2 + C\sum_{i=1}^{N}\varepsilon_i - \sum_{i=1}^{N}\alpha_i(y_i(\beta_0 + \cdots + \beta_p x_{ip}) - (1 - \varepsilon_i)) - \sum_{i=1}^{N}\mu_i\varepsilon_i$$

We want to minimize $L(x, \alpha, \mu)$.

Let's find $\nabla_x L(x, \alpha, \mu)$ and set it equal to 0.

$\frac{\partial L}{\partial \beta_j} = \beta_j - \sum_{i=1}^{N} \alpha_i y_i x_{ij}$ for $j = 1, \dots, N$

$\frac{\partial L}{\partial \beta_0} = -\sum_{i=1}^{N} \alpha_i y_i$

$\frac{\partial L}{\partial \varepsilon_j} = C - \alpha_j - \mu_j$ for $j = 1, \dots, N$

Setting $\frac{\partial L}{\partial \beta_j} = 0 \implies \beta_j = \sum_{i=1}^{N} \alpha_i y_i x_{ij}$

$$\implies \begin{bmatrix} \beta_1 \\ \vdots \\ \beta_p \end{bmatrix} = \sum_{i=1}^{N} \alpha_i y_i x_i$$

$$\implies \beta = \sum_{i=1}^{N} \alpha_i y_i x_i$$

Setting $\frac{\partial L}{\partial \beta_0} = 0 \qquad \implies \sum_{i=1}^{N} \alpha_i y_i = 0$

Setting $\frac{\partial L}{\partial \varepsilon_j} = 0 \qquad \implies \alpha_i = C - \mu_i \quad \forall i = 1, \dots, N.$

Primal feasibility requires that $g_i(x) \le 0 \; \forall i$ and $h_i(x) \le 0 \; \forall i$.

In other words, $\qquad y_i(\beta_0 + \cdots + \beta_p x_{ip}) \ge 1 - \varepsilon_i \; \forall i$

$$\varepsilon_i \ge 0 \; \forall i.$$

Dual feasibility requires that $\alpha_i \ge 0 \; \forall i$ and $\mu_i \ge 0 \; \forall i$.

Substituting the values for β and α_i into $L(x, \alpha, \mu)$, we get

$L_D(x, \alpha, \mu) = \sum_{i=1}^{N} \alpha_i - \frac{1}{2} \sum_{i=1}^{N} \sum_{j=1}^{N} \alpha_i \alpha_j y_i y_j x_i^T x_j \qquad$ (the **dual Lagrangian**)

Now, we want to find $\max\limits_{\substack{\alpha, \mu : \alpha_i \ge 0 \; \forall i \\ \mu_i \ge 0 \; \forall i}} L_D(x, \alpha, \mu)$.

Our problem now is to

$$\underset{\alpha, \mu}{maximize} \left[\sum_{i=1}^{N} \alpha_i - \frac{1}{2} \sum_{i=1}^{N} \sum_{j=1}^{N} \alpha_i \alpha_j y_i y_j x_i^T x_j \right],$$

given the constraints $\alpha_i \geq 0 \; \forall i$

$$\mu_i \geq 0 \; \forall i$$

$$\sum_{i=1}^{N} \alpha_i y_i = 0$$

$$\alpha_i = C - \mu_i \; \forall i$$

This is the same as

$$\underset{\alpha, \mu}{maximize} \left[\sum_{i=1}^{N} \alpha_i - \frac{1}{2} \sum_{i=1}^{N} \sum_{j=1}^{N} \alpha_i \alpha_j y_i y_j x_i^T x_j \right],$$

given the constraints $0 \leq \alpha_i \leq C \; \forall i$

$$\sum_{i=1}^{N} \alpha_i y_i = 0$$

$$\alpha_i = C - \mu_i \; \forall i$$

Since the function being maximized does not depend on μ, the problem is equivalent to

$$\underset{\alpha}{maximize} \left[\sum_{i=1}^{N} \alpha_i - \frac{1}{2} \sum_{i=1}^{N} \sum_{j=1}^{N} \alpha_i \alpha_j y_i y_j x_i^T x_j \right],$$

given the constraints $0 \leq \alpha_i \leq C \; \forall i$

$$\sum_{i=1}^{N} \alpha_i y_i = 0$$

THE COEFFICIENTS FOR THE SOFT MARGIN HYPERPLANE

Once this new convex optimization problem is solved for α, we can find β from $\beta = \sum_{i=1}^{N} \alpha_i y_i x_i$.

By the complementary slackness condition, $\alpha_i g_i(x) = 0 \; \forall i$ and $\mu_i h_i(x) = 0 \; \forall i$. That is,

$$\alpha_i\left(1 - \varepsilon_i - y_i(\beta_0 + \cdots + \beta_p x_{ip})\right) = 0 \ \forall i \text{ and } \mu_i \varepsilon_i = 0 \ \forall i.$$

If $\alpha_i = 0$, then $\alpha_i = C - \mu_i \implies \mu_i = C$

$$\implies \varepsilon_i = 0 \text{ since } \mu_i \varepsilon_i = 0.$$

If $\alpha_i > 0$ and $\varepsilon_i = 0$ for some i, then we can find β_0 from the equation

$$\alpha_i\left(1 - \varepsilon_i - y_i(\beta_0 + \cdots + \beta_p x_{ip})\right) = 0.$$

The nonzero ε_i can be found from the equations

$$\alpha_i\left(1 - \varepsilon_i - y_i(\beta_0 + \cdots + \beta_p x_{ip})\right) = 0 \ \forall i.$$

THE SUPPORT VECTORS (SOFT MARGIN)

Note that if $\alpha_i > 0$, then $\left(1 - \varepsilon_i - y_i(\beta_0 + \cdots + \beta_p x_{ip})\right) = 0$

$$\implies y_i(\beta_0 + \cdots + \beta_p x_{ip}) = 1 - \varepsilon_i \text{ and } x_i \text{ is called a support vector.}$$

If $y_i(\beta_0 + \cdots + \beta_p x_{ip}) > 1 - \varepsilon_i$, then $1 - \varepsilon_i - y_i(\beta_0 + \cdots + \beta_p x_{ip}) < 0$

$$\implies \alpha_i = 0 \text{ because } \alpha_i\left(1 - \varepsilon_i - y_i(\beta_0 + \cdots + \beta_p x_{ip})\right) = 0 \ \forall i,$$

$$\text{and } x_i \text{ is not relevant in } \beta = \sum_{i=1}^N \alpha_i y_i x_i.$$

β is a linear combination of only the support vectors.

CLASSIFYING TEST POINTS (SOFT MARGIN)

If we let $\hat{f}(x) = \beta_0^* + \beta_1^* x_1 + \cdots + \beta_p^* x_p$, where $x = (x_1, \ldots, x_p)$ is arbitrary in $\mathbb{R}^p$ and $(\beta_0^*, \beta_1^*, \ldots, \beta_p^*)$ is the solution to our optimization problem, then $\hat{f}(x) = \langle x, \beta^* \rangle + \beta_0^*$.

Since $\beta^* = \sum_{i=1}^N \alpha_i y_i x_i$, $\hat{f}(x) = \sum_{i=1}^N \alpha_i y_i \langle x, x_i \rangle + \beta_0^*$.

Any test point x can be classified according to the sign of $\hat{f}(x)$.

SUPPORT VECTOR CLASSIFIER EXAMPLE 1

Suppose we have the following data points:

$x_1 = (0,0), x_2 = (1,0), x_3 = (0,1), x_4 = (0,-1)$ with

$y_1 = 1, y_2 = 1, y_3 = -1, y_4 = -1.$

Find the soft margin hyperplane (with tuning parameter C=2) and identify any support vectors.

Solution:

Our convex optimization problem takes the form:

$$\underset{(\beta_0,\beta,\varepsilon)\in\mathbb{R}^7}{minimize} f(\beta_0,\beta_1,\beta_2,\varepsilon_1,\varepsilon_2,\varepsilon_3,\varepsilon_4) \qquad \text{given the constraint}$$

$$g_i(\beta_0,\beta_1,\beta_2,\varepsilon_1,\varepsilon_2,\varepsilon_3,\varepsilon_4) \leq 0 \text{ for } i = 1,2,3,4, \text{ and}$$

$$h_i(\beta_0,\beta_1,\beta_2,\varepsilon_1,\varepsilon_2,\varepsilon_3,\varepsilon_4) \leq 0 \text{ for } i = 1,2,3,4, \text{ where}$$

$$f(\beta_0,\beta,\varepsilon) = \frac{1}{2}\|\beta\|^2 + C\sum_{i=1}^{4}\varepsilon_i$$

$$g_i(\beta_0,\beta,\varepsilon) = 1 - \varepsilon_i - y_i(\beta_0 + \beta_1 x_{i1} + \beta_2 x_{i2})$$
$$\text{for } i = 1,2,3,4$$

$$h_i(\beta_0,\beta,\varepsilon) = -\varepsilon_i \text{ for } i = 1,2,3,4.$$

So $\quad g_1 = 1 - \varepsilon_1 - \beta_0$

$\quad g_2 = 1 - \varepsilon_2 - (\beta_0 + \beta_1)$

$\quad g_3 = 1 - \varepsilon_3 + (\beta_0 + \beta_2)$

$\quad g_4 = 1 - \varepsilon_4 + (\beta_0 - \beta_2)$

$\quad h_1 = -\varepsilon_1$

$\quad\quad h_2 = -\varepsilon_2$

$\quad\quad h_3 = -\varepsilon_3$

$\quad\quad h_4 = -\varepsilon_4.$

The dual Lagrangian is given by $L_D(\alpha) = \sum_{i=1}^{4}\alpha_i - \frac{1}{2}\sum_{i=1}^{4}\sum_{j=1}^{4}\alpha_i\alpha_j y_i y_j x_i^T x_j.$

So $L_D(\alpha) = (\alpha_1 + \alpha_2 + \alpha_3 + \alpha_4) - \frac{1}{2}[\alpha_2^2 + \alpha_3^2 + \alpha_4^2 - 2\alpha_3\alpha_4].$

We want to maximize $L_D(\alpha)$ subject to the constraints $0 \leq \alpha_i \leq C$ $\forall i$ and $\alpha_1 y_1 + \alpha_2 y_2 + \alpha_3 y_3 + \alpha_4 y_4 = 0$. That is, we need $0 \leq \alpha_i \leq C$ $\forall i$ and $\alpha_1 + \alpha_2 - \alpha_3 - \alpha_4 = 0$.

These constraints give us a four-dimensional plane in the positive box $0 \leq \alpha_i \leq C$ $\forall i$.

Using $\alpha_1 = -\alpha_2 + \alpha_3 + \alpha_4$, rewrite L_D as follows:

$$L_D(\alpha_2, \alpha_3, \alpha_4) = 2(\alpha_3 + \alpha_4) - \frac{1}{2}[\alpha_2^2 + \alpha_3^2 + \alpha_4^2 - 2\alpha_3\alpha_4].$$

The constraints $0 \leq \alpha_i \leq C$ $\forall i$ and $\alpha_1 = -\alpha_2 + \alpha_3 + \alpha_4$ give us a solid region inside the positive box $0 \leq \alpha_2, \alpha_3, \alpha_4 \leq C$.

$$0 \leq \alpha_1 \leq C \implies 0 \leq -\alpha_2 + \alpha_3 + \alpha_4 \leq C$$

$$\implies \alpha_2 - \alpha_3 \leq \alpha_4 \leq C + \alpha_2 - \alpha_3.$$

Let $S = \{(\alpha_2, \alpha_3, \alpha_4) | 0 \leq \alpha_2, \alpha_3, \alpha_4 \leq C \text{ and } \alpha_2 - \alpha_3 \leq \alpha_4 \leq C + \alpha_2 - \alpha_3\}$.

S looks roughly like this:

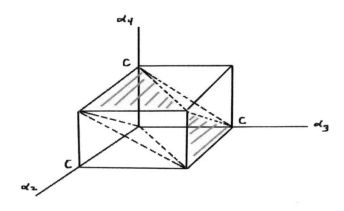

S is an 8-sided solid inside the positive box. Think of a slanted slab cutting through the positive box. S would be the intersection of the slab and the box.

We want to maximize $L_D(\alpha_2, \alpha_3, \alpha_4)$ on S.

$L_D(\alpha_2, \alpha_3, \alpha_4)$ is a continuous function on the closed and bounded region S. So to find the absolute max of L_D on S, we need to check for any critical points in S and for any extreme values of L_D on the boundary of S. The largest value of 1) the values of L_D at any critical points in S and 2) the extreme values of L_D on the boundary of S is the absolute max value.

Let's look for any critical points in the interior of S by setting $\nabla L_D = 0$.

$$\frac{\partial L_D}{\partial \alpha_2} = -\alpha_2$$

$$\frac{\partial L_D}{\partial \alpha_3} = 2 - \alpha_3 + \alpha_4$$

$$\frac{\partial L_D}{\partial \alpha_4} = 2 - \alpha_4 + \alpha_3$$

Setting $\nabla L_D = 0 \implies -\alpha_2 = 0$

$$-\alpha_3 + \alpha_4 = -2$$

$$\alpha_3 - \alpha_4 = -2$$

This system has no solution.

There is no critical point in the interior of S. We need to check the boundary of S.

The boundary of S consists of 8 faces $F_1, \ldots, F_8$ defined as follows:

$F_1 = \{(\alpha_2, \alpha_3, \alpha_4) | \alpha_2 = 0, 0 \le \alpha_3 \le C, 0 \le \alpha_4 \le C - \alpha_3\}$

$F_2 = \{(\alpha_2, \alpha_3, \alpha_4) | \alpha_2 = C, 0 \le \alpha_3 \le C, C - \alpha_3 \le \alpha_4 \le C\}$

$F_3 = \{(\alpha_2, \alpha_3, \alpha_4) | \alpha_3 = 0, 0 \le \alpha_2 \le C, \alpha_2 \le \alpha_4 \le C\}$

$F_4 = \{(\alpha_2, \alpha_3, \alpha_4) | \alpha_3 = C, 0 \le \alpha_2 \le C, 0 \le \alpha_4 \le \alpha_2\}$

$F_5 = \{(\alpha_2, \alpha_3, \alpha_4) | \alpha_4 = 0, 0 \le \alpha_2 \le C, \alpha_2 \le \alpha_3 \le C\}$

$F_6 = \{(\alpha_2, \alpha_3, \alpha_4) | \alpha_4 = C, 0 \le \alpha_2 \le C, 0 \le \alpha_3 \le \alpha_2\}$

$F_7 = \{(\alpha_2, \alpha_3, \alpha_4) | \alpha_4 = \alpha_2 - \alpha_3, 0 \le \alpha_2 \le C, 0 \le \alpha_3 \le C\}$

$F_8 = \{(\alpha_2, \alpha_3, \alpha_4) | \alpha_4 = C + \alpha_2 - \alpha_3, 0 \le \alpha_2 \le C, 0 \le \alpha_3 \le C\}$

To find the extreme values of L_D on the faces, we need to check for any critical points inside the faces and for the extreme values on the edges of each face. The calculations are tedious, and it turns out that, for $C = 2$, the maximum value of L_D is 6 and it occurs at $(\alpha_1, \alpha_2, \alpha_3, \alpha_4) = (2, 2, 2, 2)$.

$$\beta = \sum_{i=1}^{4} \alpha_i y_i x_i \implies \beta = \begin{bmatrix} 2 \\ 0 \end{bmatrix}.$$

By complementary slackness, we have $\alpha_i [1 - \varepsilon_i - y_i(\beta_0 + \beta_1 x_{i1} + \beta_2 x_{i2})] = 0 \; \forall i = 1, 2, 3, 4.$

This gives us a system of 4 equations and 5 unknowns $\varepsilon_1, \varepsilon_2, \varepsilon_3, \varepsilon_4, \beta_0$. Solving this system gives $\varepsilon_1 = 2, \varepsilon_2 = \varepsilon_3 = \varepsilon_4 = 0$, and $\beta_0 = -1$.

The equation of our hyperplane is given by $\beta_0 + \beta_1 X_1 + \beta_2 X_2 = 0$. So we get $-1 + 2X_1 = 0$

$$\Rightarrow X_1 = \frac{1}{2}.$$

Since $\alpha_i > 0$ for $i = 1, 2, 3, 4$, we have that $y_i(\beta_0 + \beta_1 x_{i1} + \beta_2 x_{i2}) = 1 - \varepsilon_i$ for each i. Hence, x_1, x_2, x_3, x_4 are all support vectors.

One last thing. What happens if we increase or decrease C? I repeated the process we just performed to the cases $C = 1$ and $C = 4$.

For $C = 4$, L_D has an absolute max value of 10 and it occurs at $(\alpha_1, \alpha_2, \alpha_3, \alpha_4) = (4, 2, 3, 3)$.

$\beta = \begin{bmatrix} 2 \\ 0 \end{bmatrix}, \beta_0 = -1, \varepsilon_1 = 2, \varepsilon_2 = \varepsilon_3 = \varepsilon_4 = 0$, and the hyperplane is $X_1 = \frac{1}{2}$, the same result we got for $C = 2$.

For $C = 1$, L_D has an absolute max value of $3\frac{1}{2}$ and it occurs at $(\alpha_1, \alpha_2, \alpha_3, \alpha_4) = (1, 1, 1, 1)$.

$\beta = \begin{bmatrix} 1 \\ 0 \end{bmatrix}$. The complementary slackness equations

$$\alpha_i[1 - \varepsilon_i - y_i(\beta_0 + \beta_1 x_{i1} + \beta_2 x_{i2})] = 0 \ \forall i = 1, 2, 3, 4$$

give us a system of 4 equations and 5 unknowns $\varepsilon_1, \varepsilon_2, \varepsilon_3, \varepsilon_4, \beta_0$. This system has more than one solution.

One solution is $\beta_0 = 0, \varepsilon_1 = 1, \varepsilon_2 = 0, \varepsilon_3 = 1, \varepsilon_4 = 1$. The hyperplane is $X_1 = 0$.

Another solution is $\beta_0 = -1, \varepsilon_1 = 2, \varepsilon_2 = 1, \varepsilon_3 = 0, \varepsilon_4 = 0$. The hyperplane is $X_1 = 1$.

SUPPORT VECTOR CLASSIFIER EXAMPLE 2

Suppose we have the following data points:

$$x_1 = (1,0), x_2 = (0,1), x_3 = (0,-1), x_4 = (0,0), x_5 = (2,0) \text{ with}$$

$$y_1 = 1, y_2 = 1, y_3 = 1, y_4 = -1, y_5 = -1.$$

Find the soft margin hyperplane (with tuning parameter C=1) and identify any support vectors.

Solution:

Our convex optimization problem takes the form:

$$\underset{(\beta_0,\beta,\varepsilon)\in\mathbb{R}^8}{minimize} f(\beta_0,\beta_1,\beta_2,\varepsilon_1,\varepsilon_2,\varepsilon_3,\varepsilon_4,\varepsilon_5) \text{ given the constraint}$$

$$g_i(\beta_0,\beta,\varepsilon) \le 0 \text{ for } i = 1, \ldots 5, \text{ and}$$

$$h_i(\beta_0,\beta,\varepsilon) \le 0 \text{ for } i = 1, \ldots 5, \text{ where}$$

$$f(\beta_0,\beta,\varepsilon) = \frac{1}{2}\|\beta\|^2 + C\sum_{i=1}^{5}\varepsilon_i$$

$$g_i(\beta_0,\beta,\varepsilon) = 1 - \varepsilon_i - y_i(\beta_0 + \beta_1 x_{i1} + \beta_2 x_{i2})$$

$$\text{for } i = 1, \ldots, 5$$

$$h_i(\beta_0,\beta,\varepsilon) = -\varepsilon_i \text{ for } i = 1, \ldots, 5.$$

So $g_1 = 1 - \varepsilon_1 - (\beta_0 + \beta_1)$

$g_2 = 1 - \varepsilon_2 - (\beta_0 + \beta_2)$

$g_3 = 1 - \varepsilon_3 - (\beta_0 - \beta_2)$

$g_4 = 1 - \varepsilon_4 + (\beta_0)$

$g_5 = 1 - \varepsilon_5 + (\beta_0 + 2\beta_1)$

$h_1 = -\varepsilon_1$

$h_2 = -\varepsilon_2$

$h_3 = -\varepsilon_3$

$h_4 = -\varepsilon_4$

$h_5 = -\varepsilon_5$

The dual Lagrangian is given by $L_D(\alpha) = \sum_{i=1}^{5} \alpha_i - \frac{1}{2}\sum_{i=1}^{5}\sum_{j=1}^{5} \alpha_i\alpha_j y_i y_j x_i^T x_j$.

So $L_D(\alpha) = (\alpha_1 + \cdots + \alpha_5) - \frac{1}{2}[\alpha_1^2 + \alpha_2^2 + \alpha_3^2 + 4\alpha_5^2 - 4\alpha_1\alpha_5 - 2\alpha_2\alpha_3]$.

We want to maximize $L_D(\alpha)$ subject to the constraints $0 \le \alpha_i \le C \ \forall i$ and $\alpha_1 y_1 + \cdots + \alpha_5 y_5 = 0$. That is, we need $0 \le \alpha_i \le C \ \forall i$ and $\alpha_1 + \alpha_2 + \alpha_3 - \alpha_4 - \alpha_5 = 0$.

These constraints give us a five-dimensional plane in the positive box $0 \le \alpha_i \le C \ \forall i$.

Let $H = \{(\alpha_1, \ldots, \alpha_5) \in \mathbb{R}^5 | 0 \le \alpha_i \le C \ \forall i \text{ and } \alpha_1 + \alpha_2 + \alpha_3 - \alpha_4 - \alpha_5 = 0\}$.

We want to maximize $L_D(\alpha_1, \ldots, \alpha_5)$ on H.

To find the maximum of $L_D(\alpha_1, \ldots, \alpha_5)$ on H, we can use any computational software.

It turns out that, for $C = 1$, the maximum value of L_D on H is $\frac{7}{2}$ and it occurs at $(\alpha_1, \ldots, \alpha_5) = (1, \frac{1}{2}, \frac{1}{2}, 1, 1)$.

$\beta = \sum_{i=1}^{5} \alpha_i y_i x_i \implies \beta = \begin{bmatrix} -1 \\ 0 \end{bmatrix}$.

By complementary slackness, we have $\alpha_i[1 - \varepsilon_i - y_i(\beta_0 + \beta_1 x_{i1} + \beta_2 x_{i2})] = 0 \ \forall i = 1, \ldots, 5$, and $\mu_i \varepsilon_i = 0 \ \forall i$.

Since $\alpha_2, \alpha_3 \ne C$ and $\alpha_i = C - \mu_i \ \forall i$, $\mu_2, \mu_3 \ne 0$. Thus, $\varepsilon_2 = \varepsilon_3 = 0$ since $\mu_i \varepsilon_i = 0 \ \forall i$.

Using $\alpha_i[1 - \varepsilon_i - y_i(\beta_0 + \beta_1 x_{i1} + \beta_2 x_{i2})] = 0 \ \forall i$, we can solve for β_0 and the remaining ε's. We get $\beta_0 = 1, \varepsilon_1 = 1, \varepsilon_2 = 0, \varepsilon_3 = 0, \varepsilon_4 = 2, \varepsilon_5 = 0$. The equation of our hyperplane is given by $\beta_0 + \beta_1 X_1 + \beta_2 X_2 = 0$. So we get $1 - X_1 = 0$

$$\implies X_1 = 1.$$

Since $\alpha_i > 0$ for $i = 1, \ldots, 5$, we have that $y_i(\beta_0 + \beta_1 x_{i1} + \beta_2 x_{i2}) = 1 - \varepsilon_i$ for each i. Hence, $x_1, \ldots, x_5$ are all support vectors.

What happens if we increase or decrease C?

If $C = 2$, L_D has an absolute max value of $\frac{13}{2}$ and it occurs at $(\alpha_1, \ldots, \alpha_5) = (2, \frac{3}{4}, \frac{3}{4}, 2, \frac{3}{2})$.

$\beta = \begin{bmatrix} -1 \\ 0 \end{bmatrix}, \beta_0 = 1, \varepsilon_1 = 1, \varepsilon_2 = 0, \varepsilon_3 = 0, \varepsilon_4 = 2, \varepsilon_5 = 0$, and the hyperplane is $X_1 = 1$, the same result we got for $C = 1$.

For $C = \frac{1}{2}$, L_D has an absolute max value of $\frac{15}{8}$ and it occurs at $(\alpha_1, \dots, \alpha_5) = \left(\frac{1}{2}, \frac{1}{4}, \frac{1}{4}, \frac{1}{2}, \frac{1}{2}\right)$.

$\beta = \begin{bmatrix} -1/2 \\ 0 \end{bmatrix}$, $\beta_0 = 1$, $\varepsilon_1 = 1/2$, $\varepsilon_2 = 0$, $\varepsilon_3 = 0$, $\varepsilon_4 = 2$, $\varepsilon_5 = 1$, and the hyperplane is $X_1 = 2$.

SUMMARY: SUPPORT VECTOR CLASSIFIER

- If the $x_i's$ are not separable by a hyperplane, we can still try to find a hyperplane that separates most of the points but that allows some violations of the margin.

- Once we find the soft margin hyperplane, we can classify new points depending on which side of the hyperplane the new point lies on.

- To find the soft margin hyperplane, we maximize the margin while penalizing violations of the margin.

- We end up with a convex optimization problem, which is solved using Lagrange multipliers.

PROBLEM SET: SUPPORT VECTOR CLASSIFIER

1. Suppose we have the following data points:

    $x_1 = (0,0), x_2 = (0,1), x_3 = (-1,0), x_4 = (1,0)$ with

    $y_1 = -1, y_2 = -1, y_3 = 1, y_4 = 1$.

    a) Find the soft margin hyperplane (with tuning parameter C=2) and identify any support vectors.

    b) Repeat with C=4.

    c) Repeat with C=1.

2. Suppose we have the following data points:

    $x_1 = (0,1), x_2 = (0,-1), x_3 = (0,0), x_4 = (1,1), x_5 = (1,-1)$ with

    $y_1 = 1, y_2 = 1, y_3 = -1, y_4 = -1, y_5 = -1$.

    a) Find the soft margin hyperplane (with tuning parameter C=2) and identify any support vectors.

    b) Repeat with C=4.

    c) Repeat with C=1.

SOLUTION SET: SUPPORT VECTOR CLASSIFIER

1. Our convex optimization problem takes the form:

$$\underset{(\beta_0,\beta,\varepsilon)\in\mathbb{R}^7}{\text{minimize}} \quad f(\beta_0,\beta_1,\beta_2,\varepsilon_1,\varepsilon_2,\varepsilon_3,\varepsilon_4) \qquad \text{given the constraint}$$

$$g_i(\beta_0,\beta,\varepsilon) \le 0 \ \text{ for } i = 1,2,3,4$$

$$\text{and } h_i(\beta_0,\beta,\varepsilon) \le 0 \text{ for } i = 1,2,3,4$$

$$\text{where } (\beta_0,\beta,\varepsilon) = \frac{1}{2}\|\beta\|^2 + C\sum_{i=1}^4 \varepsilon_i \ ,$$

$$g_i(\beta_0,\beta,\varepsilon) = 1 - \varepsilon_i - y_i(\beta_0 + \beta_1 x_{i1} + \beta_2 x_{i2}) \ \text{ for} = 1,2,3,4 \ ,$$
$$\text{and } h_i(\beta_0,\beta,\varepsilon) = -\varepsilon_i \text{ for } i = 1,2,3,4$$

So $\ g_1 = 1 - \varepsilon_1 + (\beta_0)$
$\quad g_2 = 1 - \varepsilon_2 + (\beta_0 + \beta_2)$
$\quad g_3 = 1 - \varepsilon_3 - (\beta_0 - \beta_1)$
$\quad g_4 = 1 - \varepsilon_4 - (\beta_0 + \beta_1)$
$\quad h_1 = -\varepsilon_1$
$\quad h_2 = -\varepsilon_2$
$\quad h_3 = -\varepsilon_3$
$\quad h_4 = -\varepsilon_4.$

The dual Lagrangian is given by $L_D(\alpha) = \sum_{i=1}^4 \alpha_i - \frac{1}{2}\sum_{i=1}^4\sum_{j=1}^4 \alpha_i\alpha_j y_i y_j x_i^T x_j.$

So $L_D(x,\alpha) = (\alpha_1 + \alpha_2 + \alpha_3 + \alpha_4) - \frac{1}{2}[\alpha_2^2 + \alpha_3^2 + \alpha_4^2 - 2\alpha_3\alpha_4]$

We want to maximize $L_D(\alpha)$ subject to the constraints $0 \le \alpha_i \le C \ \forall \ i$ and $\alpha_1 y_1 + \alpha_2 y_2 + \alpha_3 y_3 + \alpha_4 y_4 = 0$. That is, we need $\ 0 \le \alpha_i \le C \ \forall \ i$ and $-\alpha_1 - \alpha_2 + \alpha_3 + \alpha_4 = 0$. These constraints give us a four-dimensional plane in the positive box $0 \le \alpha_i \le C \ \forall \ i$.

Let $H = \{(\alpha_1,\dots,\alpha_4) \in \mathbb{R}^4 | 0 \le \alpha_i \le C \ \forall \ i \ and \ -\alpha_1 - \alpha_2 + \alpha_3 + \alpha_4 = 0\}$. We want to maximize $L_D(\alpha_1,\dots,\alpha_4)$ on H.

To find the maximum of $L_D(\alpha_1,\dots,\alpha_4)$ on H, we can use any computational software.

It turns out that, for $C = 2$, the maximum value of L_D on H is 6 and it occurs at $(\alpha_1,\dots,\alpha_4) = (2,2,2,2)$.

$$\beta = \sum_{i=1}^{4} \alpha_i y_i x_i$$

$$\Rightarrow \beta = \begin{bmatrix} 0 \\ -2 \end{bmatrix}.$$

By complementary slackness, we have $\alpha_i\big(1 - \varepsilon_i - y_i(\beta_0 + \beta_1 x_{i1} + \beta_2 x_{i2})\big) = 0 \ \forall \ i = 1, \dots, 4$

This gives us a system of 4 equations and 5 unknowns $\varepsilon_1, \varepsilon_2, \varepsilon_3, \varepsilon_4, \beta_0$. Solving this system gives $\varepsilon_1 = 2, \varepsilon_2 = \varepsilon_3 = \varepsilon_4 = 0$, and $\beta_0 = 1$.

The equation of our hyperplane is given by $\beta_0 + \beta_1 X_1 + \beta_2 X_2 = 0$.

So we get $1 - 2X_2 = 0$

$$\Rightarrow X_2 = \frac{1}{2}$$

Since $\alpha_i > 0$ for $i = 1, \dots, 4$, we have that each x_i satisfies $y_i(\beta_0 + \beta_1 x_{i1} + \beta_2 x_{i2}) = 1 - \varepsilon_i$. Hence, x_1, x_2, x_3, x_4 are all support vectors.

b) For $C = 4$, L_D has an absolute max value of 10 and it occurs at $(\alpha_1, \dots, \alpha_4) = (4, 2, 3, 3)$.

$\beta = \begin{bmatrix} 0 \\ -2 \end{bmatrix}, \beta_0 = 1, \varepsilon_1 = 2, \varepsilon_2 = \varepsilon_3 = \varepsilon_4 = 0$, and the hyperplane is $X_2 = \frac{1}{2}$, the same result we got for $C = 2$.

c) For $C = 1$, L_D has an absolute max value of $\frac{7}{2}$ and it occurs at $(\alpha_1, \dots, \alpha_4) = (1, 1, 1, 1)$.

$\beta = \begin{bmatrix} 0 \\ -1 \end{bmatrix}$. The complementary slackness equations

$$\alpha_i\big(1 - \varepsilon_i - y_i(\beta_0 + \beta_1 x_{i1} + \beta_2 x_{i2})\big) = 0 \ \forall \ i = 1, \dots, 4$$

give us a system of 4 equations and 5 unknowns $\varepsilon_1, \varepsilon_2, \varepsilon_3, \varepsilon_4, \beta_0$. This system has more than one solution. One solution is $\beta_0 = 0, \varepsilon_1 = 1, \varepsilon_2 = 0, \varepsilon_3 = 1, \varepsilon_4 = 1$. The hyperplane is $X_2 = 0$. Another solution is $\beta_0 = 1, \varepsilon_1 = 2, \varepsilon_2 = 1, \varepsilon_3 = 0, \varepsilon_4 = 0$. The hyperplane is $X_2 = 1$.

2. Our convex optimization problem takes the form:

$$\underset{(\beta_0, \beta, \varepsilon) \in \mathbb{R}^8}{\text{minimize}} \quad f(\beta_0, \beta_1, \beta_2, \varepsilon_1, \varepsilon_2, \varepsilon_3, \varepsilon_4, \varepsilon_5) \qquad \text{given the constraint}$$

$$g_i(\beta_0, \beta, \varepsilon) \leq 0 \ \text{ for } i = 1, 2, 3, 4, 5$$

$$\text{and } h_i(\beta_0, \beta, \varepsilon) \leq 0 \text{ for } i = 1, 2, 3, 4, 5$$

$$\text{where } (\beta_0, \beta, \varepsilon) = \frac{1}{2}\|\beta\|^2 + C\sum_{i=1}^5 \varepsilon_i \ ,$$

$$g_i(\beta_0, \beta, \varepsilon) = 1 - \varepsilon_i - y_i(\beta_0 + \beta_1 x_{i1} + \beta_2 x_{i2}) \ \text{ for } = 1, 2, 3, 4, 5,$$
$$\text{and } h_i(\beta_0, \beta, \varepsilon) = -\varepsilon_i \text{ for } i = 1, 2, 3, 4, 5$$

So $\quad g_1 = 1 - \varepsilon_1 - (\beta_0 + \beta_2)$

$\quad g_2 = 1 - \varepsilon_2 - (\beta_0 - \beta_2)$

$\quad g_3 = 1 - \varepsilon_3 + (\beta_0)$

$\quad g_4 = 1 - \varepsilon_4 + (\beta_0 + \beta_1 + \beta_2)$

$\quad g_5 = 1 - \varepsilon_5 + (\beta_0 + \beta_1 - \beta_2)$

$\quad h_1 = -\varepsilon_1$

$\quad h_2 = -\varepsilon_2$

$\quad h_3 = -\varepsilon_3$

$\quad h_4 = -\varepsilon_4$

$\quad h_5 = -\varepsilon_5$

The dual Lagrangian is given by $L_D(\alpha) = \sum_{i=1}^5 \alpha_i - \frac{1}{2}\sum_{i=1}^5 \sum_{j=1}^5 \alpha_i \alpha_j y_i y_j x_i^T x_j$.

So $L_D(x, \alpha) = (\alpha_1 + \alpha_2 + \alpha_3 + \alpha_4 + \alpha_5) - \frac{1}{2}[\alpha_1^2 + \alpha_2^2 + 2\alpha_4^2 + 2\alpha_5^2 - 2\alpha_1\alpha_2 - 2\alpha_1\alpha_4 + 2\alpha_1\alpha_5 + 2\alpha_2\alpha_4 - 2\alpha_2\alpha_5]$

We want to maximize $L_D(\alpha)$ subject to the constraints $0 \leq \alpha_i \leq C \ \forall \ i$ and $\alpha_1 y_1 + \alpha_2 y_2 + \alpha_3 y_3 + \alpha_4 y_4 + \alpha_5 y_5 = 0$. That is, we need $0 \leq \alpha_i \leq C \ \forall \ i$ and $\alpha_1 + \alpha_2 - \alpha_3 - \alpha_4 - \alpha_5 = 0$. These constraints give us a five-dimensional plane in the positive box $0 \leq \alpha_i \leq C \ \forall \ i$.

Let $H = \{(\alpha_1, ..., \alpha_4, \alpha_5) \in \mathbb{R}^5 | 0 \leq \alpha_i \leq C \ \forall \ i \ and \ \alpha_1 + \alpha_2 - \alpha_3 - \alpha_4 - \alpha_5 = 0\}$. We want to maximize $L_D(\alpha_1, ..., \alpha_4, \alpha_5)$ on H.

To find the maximum of $L_D(\alpha_1, ..., \alpha_4, \alpha_5)$ on H, we can use any computational software.

It turns out that, for $C = 2$, the maximum value of L_D on H is 6 and it occurs at $(\alpha_1, ..., \alpha_4, \alpha_5) = (2, 2, 2, 1, 1)$.

$$\beta = \sum_{i=1}^5 \alpha_i y_i x_i$$

$$\Rightarrow \beta = \begin{bmatrix} -2 \\ 0 \end{bmatrix}.$$

By complementary slackness, we have $\alpha_i\left(1 - \varepsilon_i - y_i(\beta_0 + \beta_1 x_{i1} + \beta_2 x_{i2})\right) = 0 \ \forall \ i = 1, \dots, 5$ and $\mu_i \varepsilon_i = 0 \ \forall \ i$.

Since $\alpha_4, \alpha_5 \neq C$ and $\alpha_i = C - \mu_i \ \forall \ i$, $\mu_4, \mu_5 \neq 0$. Thus, $\varepsilon_4 = \varepsilon_5 = 0$ since $\mu_i \varepsilon_i = 0 \ \forall \ i$.

Using $\alpha_i\left(1 - \varepsilon_i - y_i(\beta_0 + \beta_1 x_{i1} + \beta_2 x_{i2})\right) = 0 \ \forall \ i$, we can solve for β_0 and the remaining ε's. We get $\beta_0 = 1, \varepsilon_1 = 0, \varepsilon_2 = 0, \varepsilon_3 = 2, \varepsilon_4 = 0, \varepsilon_5 = 0$.

The equation of our hyperplane is given by $\beta_0 + \beta_1 X_1 + \beta_2 X_2 = 0$.

So we get $1 - 2X_1 = 0$

$$\Rightarrow X_1 = \frac{1}{2}$$

Since $\alpha_i > 0$ for $i = 1, \dots, 5$, we have that each x_i satisfies $y_i(\beta_0 + \beta_1 x_{i1} + \beta_2 x_{i2}) = 1 - \varepsilon_i$. Hence, x_1, x_2, x_3, x_4, x_5 are all support vectors.

b) For $C = 4$, L_D has an absolute max value of 10 and it occurs at $(\alpha_1, \dots, \alpha_5) = (4, 2, 4, 2, 0)$.

$\beta = \begin{bmatrix} -2 \\ 0 \end{bmatrix}, \beta_0 = 1, \varepsilon_1 = 0, \varepsilon_2 = 0, \varepsilon_3 = 2, \varepsilon_4 = 0, \varepsilon_5 = 0$, and the hyperplane is $X_1 = \frac{1}{2}$, the same result we got for $C = 2$.

c) For $C = 1$, L_D has an absolute max value of $\frac{7}{2}$ and it occurs at $(\alpha_1, \dots, \alpha_5) = \left(1, 1, 1, \frac{1}{2}, \frac{1}{2}\right)$.

$\beta = \begin{bmatrix} -1 \\ 0 \end{bmatrix}, \beta_0 = 0, \varepsilon_1 = 1, \varepsilon_2 = 1, \varepsilon_3 = 1, \varepsilon_4 = 0, \varepsilon_5 = 0$, and the hyperplane is $X_1 = 0$.

8 – SUPPORT VECTOR MACHINE CLASSIFIER

SUPPORT VECTOR MACHINE CLASSIFIER

So far, we have seen that we can use the maximal margin classifier to separate the two classes of data points when they are linearly separable. We have also seen that, even if the data points are not linearly separable, we can still fit a hyperplane that separates most of the points but that allows violations of the margin; we did this using the support vector classifier. If the data points are not linearly separable and it appears that the decision boundary separating the two classes is non-linear, we can use what's called the **support vector machine**, or **support vector machine classifier**. The idea is to consider a larger feature space with data points in this larger space associated with the original data points and to apply the support vector classifier to this new set of data points in the larger feature space. This will give us a linear decision boundary in the enlarged feature space but a non-linear decision boundary in the original feature space.

ENLARGING THE FEATURE SPACE

Let's make this more precise. Suppose $(x_1, y_1), \dots, (x_N, y_N)$ are our training data points. Each x_i is a p-vector in $\mathbb{R}^p$. So our feature space is $\mathbb{R}^p$. What we want to do is enlarge the feature space $\mathbb{R}^p$ by mapping each x in $\mathbb{R}^p$ to a vector in $\mathbb{R}^M$, a bigger space.

Let $h: \mathbb{R}^p \longrightarrow \mathbb{R}^M$ be defined by

$h(x) = (h_1(x), h_2(x), \dots, h_M(x))$ where $h_i: \mathbb{R}^p \longrightarrow \mathbb{R}$ are some functions.

The h_i are called basis functions.

Now consider the points $h(x_1), h(x_2), \dots, h(x_N)$ in the new feature space $\mathbb{R}^M$. Using the new training set $(h(x_1), y_1), \dots, (h(x_N), y_N)$ in the new feature space, we can apply the support vector classifier as usual and obtain a hyperplane in $\mathbb{R}^M$ that softly separates the points $h(x_1), \dots, h(x_N)$.

Recall that, in the process of solving the convex optimization problem for the support vector classifier, the dual Lagrangian was given by

$$L_D(\alpha) = \sum_{i=1}^{N} \alpha_i - \frac{1}{2} \sum_{i=1}^{N} \sum_{j=1}^{N} \alpha_i \alpha_j y_i y_j x_i^T x_j$$

Since we're using $h(x_i)$ and $h(x_j)$ instead of x_i and x_j, the dual Lagrangian becomes

$$L_D(\alpha) = \sum_{i=1}^{N} \alpha_i - \frac{1}{2} \sum_{i=1}^{N} \sum_{j=1}^{N} \alpha_i \alpha_j y_i y_j \left(h(x_i)\right)^T h(x_j)$$

$$= \sum_{i=1}^{N} \alpha_i - \frac{1}{2} \sum_{i=1}^{N} \sum_{j=1}^{N} \alpha_i \alpha_j y_i y_j \langle h(x_i), h(x_j) \rangle$$

Solving the convex optimization problem with x_i's replaced by $h(x_i)$'s gives

$\beta_j = \sum_{i=1}^{N} \alpha_i y_i \left(h(x_i)\right)_j$ for $j = 1, \dots, M$

$\Rightarrow \beta = \sum_{i=1}^{N} \alpha_i y_i h(x_i)$

If we let $\hat{f}(z) = \beta_0^* + \beta_1^* z_1 + \cdots + \beta_M^* z_M$, where $z = (z_1, \dots, z_M)$ is arbitrary in $\mathbb{R}^M$ and $(\beta_0^*, \beta_1^*, \dots, \beta_M^*)$ is the solution to our optimization problem, then $\hat{f}(z) = \langle z, \beta^* \rangle + \beta_0^*$.

Since $\beta^* = \sum_{i=1}^{N} \alpha_i y_i h(x_i)$, $\hat{f}(z) = \sum_{i=1}^{N} \alpha_i y_i \langle z, h(x_i) \rangle + \beta_0^*$.

So $\hat{f}(h(x)) = \sum_{i=1}^{N} \alpha_i y_i \langle h(x), h(x_i) \rangle + \beta_0^*$ for any $x \in \mathbb{R}^p$.

Any test point $x \in \mathbb{R}^p$ can be classified according to the sign of $\hat{f}(h(x))$. So, to classify $x \in \mathbb{R}^p$, we consider the associated point $h(x)$ in $\mathbb{R}^M$ and classify $h(x)$ using a linear decision boundary.

THE KERNEL TRICK

If we look at the solution function $\hat{f}(h(x)) = \sum_{i=1}^{N} \alpha_i y_i \langle h(x), h(x_i) \rangle + \beta_0^*$, the dot product $\langle h(x), h(x_i) \rangle$ is an instance of $K(x, x') = \langle h(x), h(x') \rangle$, what's called a ***kernel*** function. A kernel is essentially a function that can be represented as the inner product of the images of the input values under some transformation h.

For certain transformations h, the kernel function is efficiently computable. If we have $K(x, x')$ expressed in terms of x and x', we don't need to know what h looks like. Some examples of kernel functions are polynomial kernels $K(x, x') = (1 + \langle x, x' \rangle)^n$ and radial kernels $K(x, x') = e^{-\gamma \|x - x'\|^2}$. Note that we can compute these kernels by plugging in values for x and x', without knowing what the transformation h is.

Now, instead of constructing a transformation h explicitly, and computing the dot products $\langle h(x), h(x_i) \rangle$, we can replace the dot products that occur in the dual Lagrangian and the solution function $\hat{f}$ with kernels like so:

$$L_D(\alpha) = \sum_{i=1}^{N} \alpha_i - \frac{1}{2}\sum_{i=1}^{N}\sum_{j=1}^{N}\alpha_i\alpha_j y_i y_j K(x_i, x_j)$$

$$\hat{f}(x) = \sum_{i=1}^{N}\alpha_i y_i K(x, x_i) + \beta_0^* \text{ for any } x \in \mathbb{R}^p.$$

This replacement is called the **kernel trick**.

Any test point $x \in \mathbb{R}^p$ can be classified according to the sign of $\hat{f}(x)$. This is how the support vector machine classifies points in $\mathbb{R}^p$. The kernel K should be a **valid kernel**; that is, there should be a feature space mapping h that corresponds to K. By Mercer's theorem, it's sufficient that K be symmetric positive semidefinite.

In the support vector machine method, the enlarged feature space could be very high-dimensional, even infinite dimensional. By working directly with kernels, we don't have to deal with the feature mapping h or the enlarged feature space.

SUPPORT VECTOR MACHINE CLASSIFIER EXAMPLE 1

Suppose we have the following data points:

$x_1 = (0,0), x_2 = (1,1), x_3 = (1,-1), x_4 = (1,0), x_5 = (2,0)$ with

$y_1 = 1, y_2 = 1, y_3 = 1, y_4 = -1, y_5 = -1.$

a) Find the SVM decision boundary (with tuning parameter $C = 4$) using the second-degree polynomial kernel $K(x_i, x_j) = (1 + \langle x_i, x_j \rangle)^2$ and identify any support vectors.

b) Repeat with $C = 8$.

c) Repeat with $C = 2$.

Solution:

The dual Lagrangian is given by

$$L_D(\alpha) = \sum_{i=1}^{5} \alpha_i - \frac{1}{2}\sum_{i=1}^{5}\sum_{j=1}^{5}\alpha_i\alpha_j y_i y_j K(x_i, x_j)$$

So $L_D(\alpha) = (\alpha_1 + \cdots + \alpha_5) - \frac{1}{2}[\alpha_1^2 + 9\alpha_2^2 + 9\alpha_3^2 + 4\alpha_4^2 + 25\alpha_5^2 + 2(\alpha_1\alpha_2 + \alpha_1\alpha_3 + \alpha_2\alpha_3 - \alpha_1\alpha_4 - 4\alpha_2\alpha_4 - 4\alpha_3\alpha_4 - \alpha_1\alpha_5 - 9\alpha_2\alpha_5 - 9\alpha_3\alpha_5 + 9\alpha_4\alpha_5)]$

We want to maximize $L_D(\alpha)$ subject to the constraints $0 \le \alpha_i \le C$ $\forall i$ and $\alpha_1 y_1 + \cdots + \alpha_5 y_5 = 0$. That is, we need $0 \le \alpha_i \le C$ $\forall i$ and $\alpha_1 + \alpha_2 + \alpha_3 - \alpha_4 - \alpha_5 = 0$. These constraints give us a five-dimensional plane in the positive box $0 \le \alpha_i \le C$ $\forall i$.

Let $H = \{(\alpha_1, \ldots, \alpha_5) \in \mathbb{R}^5 | 0 \le \alpha_i \le C \ \forall i \ and \ \alpha_1 + \alpha_2 + \alpha_3 - \alpha_4 - \alpha_5 = 0\}$. We want to maximize $L_D(\alpha_1, \ldots, \alpha_5)$ on H. To find the maximum of $L_D(\alpha_1, \ldots, \alpha_5)$ on H, we can use any computational software.

It turns out that, for $C = 4$, the maximum value of L_D on H is $\frac{8}{3}$ and it occurs at $(\alpha_1, \ldots, \alpha_5) = \left(\frac{2}{3}, 1, 1, \frac{8}{3}, 0\right)$.

If $0 < \alpha_i < C$ $\implies \mu_i = C - \alpha_i > 0$ because $\alpha_i < C$

$\implies \varepsilon_i = 0$ because $\mu_i \varepsilon_i = 0$

By complementary slackness, we have

$\alpha_i [1 - \varepsilon_i - y_i \hat{f}(x_i)] = 0$ where $\hat{f}(x) = \sum_{i=1}^{5} \alpha_i y_i K(x, x_i) + \beta_0^*$ $\quad \forall x \in \mathbb{R}^2$

$\implies \alpha_i [1 - y_i \hat{f}(x_i)] = 0$ because $\varepsilon_i = 0$ for $0 < \alpha_i < C$

$\implies 1 - y_i \hat{f}(x_i) = 0$ because $\alpha_i > 0$

$\implies y_i \hat{f}(x_i) = 1$

This equation will allow us to find β_0^*.

For $C = 4$, $0 < \alpha_1 < C$ $\implies y_1 \hat{f}(x_1) = 1$

$\implies \hat{f}(x_1) = 1$

$\implies \sum_{i=1}^{5} \alpha_i y_i K(x_1, x_i) + \beta_0^* = 1$

$\implies \frac{2}{3} K(x_1, x_1) + K(x_1, x_2) + K(x_1, x_3) - \frac{8}{3} K(x_1, x_4) - 0 \cdot K(x_1, x_5) + \beta_0^* = 1$

$\implies \frac{2}{3} + 1 + 1 - \frac{8}{3} + \beta_0^* = 1$

$\implies \beta_0^* = 1$

So $\hat{f}(x) = \frac{2}{3} K(x, x_1) + K(x, x_2) + K(x, x_3) - \frac{8}{3} K(x, x_4) + 1$

$= \frac{2}{3} + (1 + X_1 + X_2)^2 + (1 + X_1 - X_2)^2 - \frac{8}{3}(1 + X_1)^2 + 1$

$= \frac{1}{3}(3 - 4X_1 - 2X_1^2 + 6X_2^2)$

Points are classified according to the sign of $\hat{f}(x)$. Setting $\hat{f}(x) = 0$ gives us a curve in the plane.

$$\hat{f}(x) = 0 \quad \Rightarrow \quad 3 - 4X_1 - 2X_1^2 + 6X_2^2 = 0$$

This gives us a hyperbola in the plane.

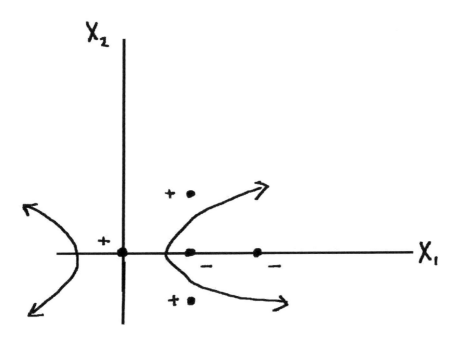

Since $\alpha_i > 0$ for $i = 1, \dots, 4$, we have that $y_i \hat{f}(x_i) = 1 - \varepsilon_i$ for $i = 1, \dots, 4$. Hence, $x_1, \dots, x_4$ are support vectors.

b) If $C = 8$, L_D has a maximum value of $\frac{8}{3}$ and it occurs at $(\alpha_1, \dots, \alpha_5) = \left(\frac{2}{3}, 1, 1, \frac{8}{3}, 0\right)$, the same result we got for $C = 4$. The decision boundary is the same hyperbola we got for $C = 4$.

c) For $C = 2$, L_D has a maximum value of $\frac{5}{2}$ and it occurs at $(\alpha_1, \dots, \alpha_5) = \left(\frac{1}{2}, \frac{3}{4}, \frac{3}{4}, 2, 0\right)$.

For $C = 2, 0 < \alpha_1 < C \quad \Rightarrow \quad y_1 \hat{f}(x_1) = 1$

$$\Rightarrow \hat{f}(x_1) = 1$$

$$\Rightarrow \sum_{i=1}^{5} \alpha_i y_i K(x_1, x_i) + \beta_0^* = 1$$

$$\Rightarrow \frac{1}{2} K(x_1, x_1) + \frac{3}{4} K(x_1, x_2) + \frac{3}{4} K(x_1, x_3) - 2K(x_1, x_4) + \beta_0^* = 1$$

$$\Rightarrow \frac{1}{2} + \frac{3}{4} + \frac{3}{4} - 2 + \beta_0^* = 1$$

$$\Rightarrow \beta_0^* = 1$$

So $\hat{f}(x) = \frac{1}{2} + \frac{3}{4}(1 + X_1 + X_2)^2 + \frac{3}{4}(1 + X_1 - X_2)^2 - 2(1 + X_1)^2 + 1$

$$= \frac{1}{2}(2 - 2X_1 - X_1^2 + 3X_2^2)$$

Setting $\hat{f}(x) = 0 \implies 2 - 2X_1 - X_1^2 + 3X_2^2 = 0$

This gives us a hyperbola in the plane.

Since $\alpha_i > 0$ for $i = 1, \dots, 4$, $x_1, \dots, x_4$ are support vectors.

SUPPORT VECTOR MACHINE CLASSIFIER EXAMPLE 2

Suppose we have the following data points:

$x_1 = (0,0), x_2 = (1,1), x_3 = (1,-1), x_4 = (1,0), x_5 = (2,0)$ with

$y_1 = 1, y_2 = 1, y_3 = 1, y_4 = -1, y_5 = -1.$

a) Find the SVM decision boundary (with tuning parameter $C = 4$) using the radial kernel

$K(x_i, x_j) = e^{-\|x_i - x_j\|^2}$ and identify any support vectors.

b) Repeat with $C = 8$.

c) Repeat with $C = 2$.

Solution:

The dual Lagrangian is given by

$$L_D(\alpha) = \sum_{i=1}^{5} \alpha_i - \frac{1}{2}\sum_{i=1}^{5}\sum_{j=1}^{5} \alpha_i \alpha_j y_i y_j K(x_i, x_j)$$

So $L_D(\alpha) = (\alpha_1 + \dots + \alpha_5) - \frac{1}{2}[\alpha_1^2 + \alpha_2^2 + \alpha_3^2 + \alpha_4^2 + \alpha_5^2 + 2(e^{-2}\alpha_1\alpha_2 + e^{-2}\alpha_1\alpha_3 - e^{-1}\alpha_1\alpha_4 - e^{-4}\alpha_1\alpha_5 + e^{-4}\alpha_2\alpha_3 - e^{-1}\alpha_2\alpha_4 - e^{-2}\alpha_2\alpha_5 - e^{-1}\alpha_3\alpha_4 - e^{-2}\alpha_3\alpha_5 + e^{-1}\alpha_4\alpha_5)]$

We want to maximize $L_D(\alpha)$ subject to the constraints $0 \le \alpha_i \le C$ $\forall i$ and $\alpha_1 y_1 + \dots + \alpha_5 y_5 = 0$. That is, we need $0 \le \alpha_i \le C$ $\forall i$ and $\alpha_1 + \alpha_2 + \alpha_3 - \alpha_4 - \alpha_5 = 0$. These constraints give us a five-dimensional plane in the positive box $0 \le \alpha_i \le C$ $\forall i$.

Let $H = \{(\alpha_1, \dots, \alpha_5) \in \mathbb{R}^5 | 0 \le \alpha_i \le C \; \forall i \text{ and } \alpha_1 + \alpha_2 + \alpha_3 - \alpha_4 - \alpha_5 = 0\}$. We want to maximize $L_D(\alpha_1, \dots, \alpha_5)$ on H. To find the maximum of $L_D(\alpha_1, \dots, \alpha_5)$ on H, we can use any computational software.

It turns out that, for $C = 4$, the maximum value of L_D on H is 3.6 and it occurs at $(\alpha_1, \dots, \alpha_5) = (0.989, 1.3, 1.3, 2.55, 1.048)$.

For $C = 4, 0 < \alpha_1 < C \quad \Rightarrow \quad y_1 \hat{f}(x_1) = 1$

$$\Rightarrow \hat{f}(x_1) = 1$$

$$\Rightarrow \sum_{i=1}^{5} \alpha_i y_i K(x_1, x_i) + \beta_0^* = 1$$

$$\Rightarrow 0.989 + 1.3e^{-2} + 1.3e^{-2} - 2.55e^{-1} - 1.048e^{-4} + \beta_0^* = 1$$

$$\Rightarrow \beta_0^* = 0.616$$

So $\hat{f}(x) = 0.989e^{-\|x-x_1\|^2} + 1.3e^{-\|x-x_2\|^2} + 1.3e^{-\|x-x_3\|^2} - 2.55e^{-\|x-x_4\|^2} - 1.048e^{-\|x-x_5\|^2} + 0.616$

$$= 0.989e^{-[x_1^2+x_2^2]} + 1.3e^{-[(x_1-1)^2+(x_2-1)^2]} + 1.3e^{-[(x_1-1)^2+(x_2+1)^2]} - 2.55e^{-[(x_1-1)^2+x_2^2]} -$$
$1.048e^{-[(x_1-2)^2+x_2^2]} + 0.616$

Setting $\hat{f}(x) = 0$ gives us a curve in the plane.

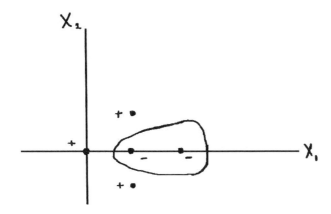

$\hat{f}(x) > 0$ corresponds to outside the loop.

$\hat{f}(x) < 0$ corresponds to inside the loop.

Since $\alpha_i > 0$ for $i = 1, \dots, 5$, each x_i is a support vector.

b) If $C = 8$, L_D has a maximum value of 3.6 and it occurs at $(\alpha_1, \dots, \alpha_5) = (0.989, 1.3, 1.3, 2.55, 1.048)$, the same result we got for $C = 4$. The decision boundary is the same loop we got for $C = 4$.

c) For $C = 2$, L_D has a maximum value of 3.51 and it occurs at $(\alpha_1, \dots, \alpha_5) = (0.849, 1.168, 1.168, 2, 1.187)$.

For $C = 2, 0 < \alpha_1 < C \quad \Rightarrow \quad y_1 \hat{f}(x_1) = 1$

$$\Rightarrow \hat{f}(x_1) = 1$$

$$\Rightarrow \sum_{i=1}^{5} \alpha_i y_i K(x_1, x_i) + \beta_0^* = 1$$

$$\Rightarrow 0.849 + 1.168e^{-2} + 1.168c^{-2} - 2e^{-1} - 1.187e^{-4} + \beta_0^* = 1$$

$$\Rightarrow \beta_0^* = 0.59$$

So $\hat{f}(x) = 0.849e^{-\|x-x_1\|^2} + 1.168e^{-\|x-x_2\|^2} + 1.168e^{-\|x-x_3\|^2} - 2e^{-\|x-x_4\|^2} - 1.187e^{-\|x-x_5\|^2} + 0.59$

$$= 0.849e^{-[x_1^2 + x_2^2]} + 1.168e^{-[(x_1-1)^2 + (x_2-1)^2]} + 1.168e^{-[(x_1-1)^2 + (x_2+1)^2]} - 2e^{-[(x_1-1)^2 + x_2^2]} -$$
$$1.187e^{-[(x_1-2)^2 + x_2^2]} + 0.59$$

Setting $\hat{f}(x) = 0$ gives us a curve in the plane. It's a loop very similar to the one for $C = 4$.

Since $\alpha_i > 0$ for $i = 1, \dots, 5$, each x_i is a support vector.

SUMMARY: SUPPORT VECTOR MACHINE CLASSIFIER

- If the x_i's of our data are not linearly separable and the decision boundary appears to be non-linear, we can find a non-linear decision boundary using the support vector machine.

- We embed the data points in a larger feature space and apply the support vector classifier to this new set of data points to get a linear decision boundary in the larger space. Any new point is classified by sending it into the larger space and using the linear decision boundary.

- The dot products that occur in the dual Lagrangian and the solution function $\hat{f}$ are replaced by a kernel K. This is called the kernel trick.

- By working directly with kernels, we can take advantage of an enlarged feature space that is very high-dimensional, perhaps even infinite dimensional, without having to deal explicitly with the feature mapping h or the enlarged feature space.

PROBLEM SET: SUPPORT VECTOR MACHINE CLASSIFIER

1. Suppose we have the following data points:

   $x_1 = (0,0), x_2 = (2,0), x_3 = (1,0), x_4 = (1,1), x_5 = (1,-1)$ with

   $y_1 = -1, y_2 = -1, y_3 = 1, y_4 = 1, y_5 = 1.$

   a) Find the SVM decision boundary (with tuning parameter C=4) using the second-degree

   polynomial kernel $K(x_i, x_j) = (1 + \langle x_i, x_j \rangle)^2$ and identify any support vectors.

   b) Repeat with C=8.

   c) Repeat with C=2.

2. Suppose we have the following data points:

   $x_1 = (0,0), x_2 = (2,0), x_3 = (1,0), x_4 = (1,1), x_5 = (1,-1)$ with

   $y_1 = -1, y_2 = -1, y_3 = 1, y_4 = 1, y_5 = 1.$

   a) Find the SVM decision boundary (with tuning parameter C=2) using the radial kernel

   $K(x_i, x_j) = e^{-\|x_i - x_j\|^2}$ and identify any support vectors.

   b) Repeat with C=4.

   c) Repeat with C=1.

SOLUTION SET: SUPPORT VECTOR MACHINE CLASSIFIER

1. a) The dual Lagrangian is given by

$$L_D(\alpha) = \sum_{i=1}^{5} \alpha_i - \frac{1}{2} \sum_{i=1}^{5} \sum_{j=1}^{5} \alpha_i \alpha_j y_i y_j K(x_i, x_j)$$

So $L_D(\alpha) = (\alpha_1 + \cdots + \alpha_5) - \frac{1}{2}[\alpha_1^2 + 25\alpha_2^2 + 4\alpha_3^2 + 9\alpha_4^2 + 9\alpha_5^2 + 2(\alpha_1\alpha_2 - \alpha_1\alpha_3 - \alpha_1\alpha_4 - \alpha_1\alpha_5 - 9\alpha_2\alpha_3 - 9\alpha_2\alpha_4 - 9\alpha_2\alpha_5 + 4\alpha_3\alpha_4 + 4\alpha_3\alpha_5 + \alpha_4\alpha_5)]$

We want to maximize $L_D(\alpha)$ subject to the constraints $0 \le \alpha_i \le C \ \forall i$ and $\alpha_1 y_1 + \cdots + \alpha_5 y_5 = 0$. That is, we need $0 \le \alpha_i \le C \ \forall i$ and $-\alpha_1 - \alpha_2 + \alpha_3 + \alpha_4 + \alpha_5 = 0$. These constraints give us a five-dimensional plane in the positive box $0 \le \alpha_i \le C \ \forall i$.

Let $H = \{(\alpha_1, \ldots, \alpha_5) \in \mathbb{R}^5 | 0 \le \alpha_i \le C \ \forall i \ and \ -\alpha_1 - \alpha_2 + \alpha_3 + \alpha_4 + \alpha_5 = 0\}$. We want to maximize $L_D(\alpha_1, \ldots, \alpha_5)$ on H. To find the maximum of $L_D(\alpha_1, \ldots, \alpha_5)$ on H, we can use any computational software.

It turns out that, for $C = 4$, the maximum value of L_D on H is $\frac{11}{2}$ and it occurs at $(\alpha_1, \ldots, \alpha_5) = \left(3, \frac{3}{2}, 4, \frac{1}{4}, \frac{1}{4}\right)$.

For $C = 4, 0 < \alpha_1 < C \quad \Rightarrow \quad y_1 \hat{f}(x_1) = 1$

$$\Rightarrow \hat{f}(x_1) = -1$$

$$\Rightarrow \sum_{i=1}^{5} \alpha_i y_i K(x_1, x_i) + \beta_0^* = -1$$

$$\Rightarrow -3K(x_1, x_1) - \frac{3}{2}K(x_1, x_2) + 4K(x_1, x_3) + \frac{1}{4}K(x_1, x_4) + \frac{1}{4}K(x_1, x_5) + \beta_0^* = -1$$

$$\Rightarrow -3 - \frac{3}{2} + 4 + \frac{1}{4} + \frac{1}{4} + \beta_0^* = -1$$

$$\Rightarrow \beta_0^* = -1$$

So $\hat{f}(x) = -3K(x, x_1) - \frac{3}{2}K(x, x_2) + 4K(x, x_3) + \frac{1}{4}K(x, x_4) + \frac{1}{4}K(x, x_5) - 1$

$$= -3 - \frac{3}{2}(1 + 2X_1)^2 + 4(1 + X_1)^2 + \frac{1}{4}(1 + X_1 + X_2)^2 + \frac{1}{4}(1 + X_1 - X_2)^2 - 1$$

$$= \frac{1}{2}(-2 + 6X_1 - 3X_1^2 + X_2^2)$$

Points are classified according to the sign of $\hat{f}(x)$. Setting $\hat{f}(x) = 0$ gives us a curve in the plane.

$\hat{f}(x) = 0 \quad \Rightarrow \quad -2 + 6X_1 - 3X_1^2 + X_2^2 = 0$

This gives us a hyperbola in the plane.

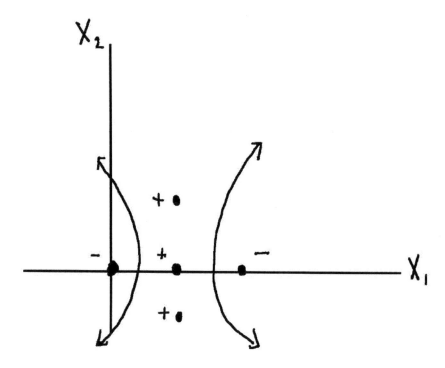

Since $\alpha_i > 0$ for $i = 1, \dots, 5$, we have that $x_1, \dots, x_5$ are support vectors.

b) For $C = 8$, L_D has a maximum value of 6 and it occurs at $(\alpha_1, \dots, \alpha_5) = (4,2,6,0,0)$.

For $C = 8, 0 < \alpha_1 < C \quad \Rightarrow \quad y_1\hat{f}(x_1) = 1$

$$\Rightarrow \hat{f}(x_1) = -1$$

$$\Rightarrow \sum_{i=1}^{5} \alpha_i y_i K(x_1, x_i) + \beta_0^* = -1$$

$$\Rightarrow -4K(x_1, x_1) - 2K(x_1, x_2) + 6K(x_1, x_3) + 0K(x_1, x_4) + 0K(x_1, x_5) + \beta_0^* = -1$$

$$\Rightarrow -4 - 2 + 6 + 0 + 0 + \beta_0^* = -1$$

$$\Rightarrow \beta_0^* = -1$$

So $\hat{f}(x) = -4 - 2(1 + 2X_1)^2 + 6(1 + X_1)^2 - 1$

$$= -1 + 4X_1 - 2X_1^2$$

Setting $\hat{f}(x) = 0 \Longrightarrow -1 + 4X_1 - 2X_1^2 = 0$

This gives us two vertical lines in the plane.

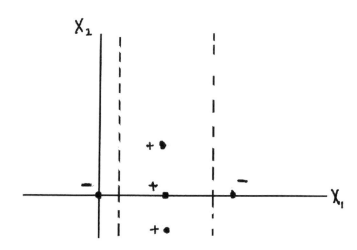

Since $\alpha_i > 0$ for $i = 1, 2, 3$, we have that x_1, x_2, x_3 are support vectors. Since x_4 and x_5 satisfy $y_i \hat{f}(x_i) = 1 - \varepsilon_i$, x_4 and x_5 are also support vectors.

c) For $C = 2$, L_D has a maximum value of 4 and it occurs at $(\alpha_1, \ldots, \alpha_5) = \left(2, 1, 2, \frac{1}{2}, \frac{1}{2}\right)$.

For $C = 2$, $0 < \alpha_2 < C \Longrightarrow y_2 \hat{f}(x_2) = 1$

$$\Longrightarrow \hat{f}(x_2) = -1$$

$$\Longrightarrow \sum_{i=1}^{5} \alpha_i y_i K(x_2, x_i) + \beta_0^* = -1$$

$$\Longrightarrow -2K(x_2, x_1) - K(x_2, x_2) + 2K(x_2, x_3) + \frac{1}{2}K(x_2, x_4) + \frac{1}{2}K(x_2, x_5) + \beta_0^* = -1$$

$$\Longrightarrow -2 - 25 + 2 \cdot 9 + \frac{1}{2} \cdot 9 + \frac{1}{2} \cdot 9 + \beta_0^* = -1$$

$$\Longrightarrow \beta_0^* = -1$$

So $\hat{f}(x) = -2 - (1 + 2X_1)^2 + 2(1 + X_1)^2 + \frac{1}{2}(1 + X_1 + X_2)^2 + \frac{1}{2}(1 + X_1 - X_2)^2 - 1$

$$= -1 + 2X_1 - X_1^2 + X_2^2$$

Setting $\hat{f}(x) = 0 \Longrightarrow -1 + 2X_1 - X_1^2 + X_2^2 = 0$

This gives us two lines in the plane, $X_2 = X_1 - 1$ and $X_2 = -X_1 + 1$.

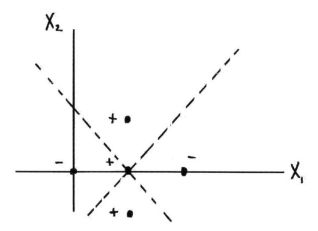

Since $\alpha_i > 0$ for $i = 1, \dots, 5$, $x_1, \dots, x_5$ are all support vectors.

2. a) The dual Lagrangian is given by

$$L_D(\alpha) = \sum_{i=1}^{5} \alpha_i - \frac{1}{2}\sum_{i=1}^{5}\sum_{j=1}^{5} \alpha_i \alpha_j y_i y_j K(x_i, x_j)$$

So $L_D(\alpha) = (\alpha_1 + \cdots + \alpha_5) - \frac{1}{2}[\alpha_1^2 + \alpha_2^2 + \alpha_3^2 + \alpha_4^2 + \alpha_5^2 + 2(e^{-4}\alpha_1\alpha_2 - e^{-1}\alpha_1\alpha_3 - e^{-2}\alpha_1\alpha_4 - e^{-2}\alpha_1\alpha_5 - e^{-1}\alpha_2\alpha_3 - e^{-2}\alpha_2\alpha_4 - e^{-2}\alpha_2\alpha_5 + e^{-1}\alpha_3\alpha_4 + e^{-1}\alpha_3\alpha_5 + e^{-4}\alpha_4\alpha_5)]$

We want to maximize $L_D(\alpha)$ subject to the constraints $0 \le \alpha_i \le C$ $\forall i$ and $\alpha_1 y_1 + \cdots + \alpha_5 y_5 = 0$. That is, we need $0 \le \alpha_i \le C$ $\forall i$ and $-\alpha_1 - \alpha_2 + \alpha_3 + \alpha_4 + \alpha_5 = 0$. These constraints give us a five-dimensional plane in the positive box $0 \le \alpha_i \le C$ $\forall i$.

Let $H = \{(\alpha_1, \dots, \alpha_5) \in \mathbb{R}^5 | 0 \le \alpha_i \le C \; \forall i \text{ and } -\alpha_1 - \alpha_2 + \alpha_3 + \alpha_4 + \alpha_5 = 0\}$. We want to maximize $L_D(\alpha_1, \dots, \alpha_5)$ on H. To find the maximum of $L_D(\alpha_1, \dots, \alpha_5)$ on H, we can use any computational software.

It turns out that, for $C = 2$, the maximum value of L_D on H is 3.52 and it occurs at $(\alpha_1, \dots, \alpha_5) = (1.76, 1.76, 1.7, 0.91, 0.91)$.

For $C = 2$, $0 < \alpha_1 < C \;\; \Rightarrow \; y_1 \hat{f}(x_1) = 1$

$\Rightarrow \; \hat{f}(x_1) = -1$

$\Rightarrow \; \Sigma_{i=1}^{5} \alpha_i y_i K(x_1, x_i) + \beta_0^* = -1$

$\Rightarrow \; -1.76 - 1.76e^{-4} + 1.7e^{-1} + 0.91e^{-2} + 0.91e^{-2} + \beta_0^* = -1$

$\Rightarrow \; \beta_0^* = -0.077$

So

$$\hat{f}(x) = -1.76e^{-\|x-x_1\|^2} - 1.76e^{-\|x-x_2\|^2} + 1.7e^{-\|x-x_3\|^2} + 0.91e^{-\|x-x_4\|^2} + 0.91e^{-\|x-x_5\|^2} - 0.077$$

$$= -1.76e^{-[X_1^2+X_2^2]} - 1.76e^{-[(X_1-2)^2+X_2^2]} + 1.7e^{-[(X_1-1)^2+X_2^2]} + 0.91e^{-[(X_1-1)^2+(X_2-1)^2]} +$$
$$0.91e^{-[(X_1-1)^2+(X_2+1)^2]} - 0.077$$

Setting $\hat{f}(x) = 0$ gives us a curve in the plane.

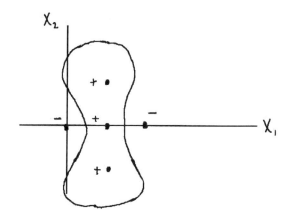

$\hat{f}(x) > 0$ corresponds to inside the peanut-like loop.

$\hat{f}(x) < 0$ corresponds to outside the peanut-like loop.

Since $\alpha_i > 0$ for $i = 1, \dots, 5$, each x_i is a support vector.

b) If $C = 4$, L_D has a maximum value of 3.52 and it occurs at $(\alpha_1, \dots, \alpha_5) =$ $(1.76, 1.76, 1.7, 0.91, 0.91)$, the same result we got for $C = 2$. The decision boundary is the same peanut-like loop we got for $C = 2$.

c) For $C = 1$, L_D has a maximum value of 2.86 and it occurs at $(\alpha_1, \dots, \alpha_5) = (1, 1, 0.96, 0.51, 0.51)$.

$$\text{For } C = 1, 0 < \alpha_3 < C \implies y_3\hat{f}(x_3) = 1$$

$$\implies \hat{f}(x_3) = 1$$

$$\implies \sum_{i=1}^{5} \alpha_i y_i K(x_3, x_i) + \beta_0^* = 1$$

$$\implies -e^{-1} - e^{-1} + 0.96 + 0.51e^{-1} + 0.51e^{-1} + \beta_0^* = 1$$

$$\implies \beta_0^* = 0.388$$

So $\hat{f}(x) = -e^{-\|x-x_1\|^2} - e^{-\|x-x_2\|^2} + 0.96e^{-\|x-x_3\|^2} + 0.51e^{-\|x-x_4\|^2} + 0.51e^{-\|x-x_5\|^2} + 0.388$

$$= -e^{-[X_1^2+X_2^2]} - e^{-[(X_1-2)^2+X_2^2]} + 0.96e^{-[(X_1-1)^2+X_2^2]} + 0.51e^{-[(X_1-1)^2+(X_2-1)^2]} +$$
$$0.51e^{-[(X_1-1)^2+(X_2+1)^2]} + 0.388$$

Setting $\hat{f}(x) = 0$ gives us a pair of loops in the plane.

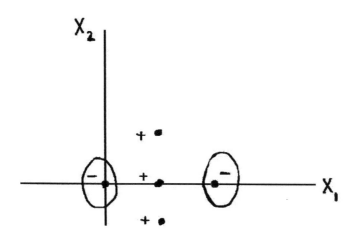

$\hat{f}(x) > 0$ corresponds to the region outside the loop.

$\hat{f}(x) < 0$ corresponds to the regions inside the loops.

Since $\alpha_i > 0$ for $i = 1, \dots, 5$, each x_i is a support vector.

CONCLUSION

Congratulations on completing the Math for Machine Learning book! Here is a review of what we have covered in this course:

- **Linear Regression**

- **Linear Discriminant Analysis**

- **Logistic Regression**

- **Artificial Neural Networks**

- **Support Vector Machines**

I hope this book has been useful to you, and I wish you the best in your career and future endeavors. If you feel that you've benefitted from this course, I'd really appreciate it if you wrote a short review for the book.

Be sure to get the companion online course Math for Machine Learning here: Math for Machine Learning Online Course. For more online courses, visit: Online Math Training.

Thank you, again!

Richard Han

APPENDIX 1

Claim: The perpendicular distance between x_i and the separating hyperplane $\beta_0 + \beta_1 X_1 + \cdots + \beta_p X_p = 0$ is given by $\frac{1}{\|\beta\|} y_i(\beta_0 + \beta_1 x_{i1} + \cdots + \beta_p x_{ip})$.

Proof: The hyperplane $\beta_0 + \beta_1 X_1 + \cdots + \beta_p X_p = 0$ can be rewritten as $\beta_1 X_1 + \cdots + \beta_p X_p = -\beta_0$. So the normal vector is $\boldsymbol{n} = \frac{1}{\|\beta\|}(\beta_1, \dots, \beta_p)$.

Let L denote the hyperplane. Let x_0 be the vector where L and the normal line intersect. Let x be an arbitrary point.

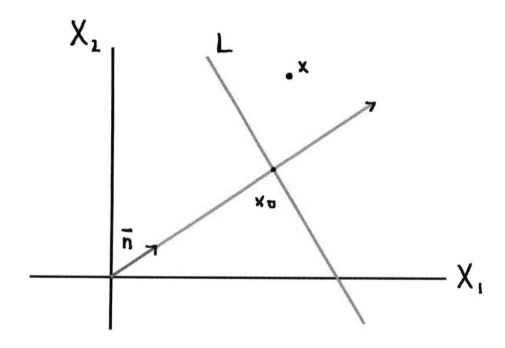

Let $\boldsymbol{z} = x - x_0$ and let $\boldsymbol{u}$ be the orthogonal projection of x onto L. Let $\boldsymbol{v} = \boldsymbol{z} - \boldsymbol{u}.$

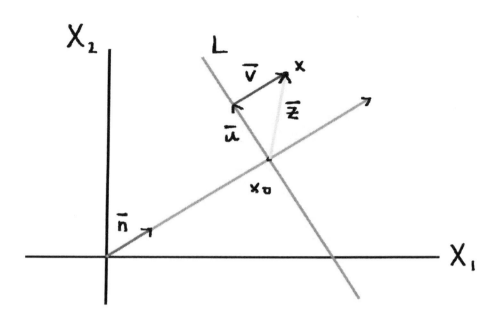

Note that $\mathbf{n} \cdot \mathbf{u} = 0$.

$\Rightarrow \ \mathbf{n} \cdot (\mathbf{z} - \mathbf{v}) = 0$

$\Rightarrow \ \mathbf{n} \cdot (x - x_0 - \mathbf{v}) = 0$

$\Rightarrow \ \mathbf{n} \cdot (x - x_0 - k\mathbf{n}) = 0 \qquad$ because $\mathbf{v} = k\mathbf{n}$ for some scalar k.

$\Rightarrow \ \mathbf{n} \cdot (x - x_0) - k\mathbf{n} \cdot \mathbf{n} = 0$

$\Rightarrow \ \mathbf{n} \cdot (x - x_0) - k = 0$

$\Rightarrow \ k = \mathbf{n} \cdot (x - x_0)$

The distance between x and L is $\|\mathbf{v}\| = |k| \|\mathbf{n}\| = |k|$.

So $\|\mathbf{v}\| = |k| = |\mathbf{n} \cdot (x - x_0)|$

$\qquad = |\mathbf{n} \cdot x - \mathbf{n} \cdot x_0|$

$\qquad = \left| \mathbf{n} \cdot x - \left(-\dfrac{\beta_0}{\|\beta\|} \right) \right| \quad$ because x_0 lies on $L \ \Rightarrow \beta_0 + \beta_1 x_{01} + \cdots + \beta_p x_{0p} = 0$

$\qquad\qquad\qquad\qquad\qquad\qquad\qquad \Rightarrow \beta_0 + \|\beta\| \mathbf{n} \cdot x_0 = 0$

$\qquad\qquad\qquad\qquad\qquad\qquad\qquad \Rightarrow \mathbf{n} \cdot x_0 = -\dfrac{\beta_0}{\|\beta\|}$

$\qquad = \left| \mathbf{n} \cdot x + \left(\dfrac{\beta_0}{\|\beta\|} \right) \right|$

135

Therefore, the perpendicular distance between x_i and the hyperplane $\beta_0 + \beta_1 X_1 + \cdots + \beta_p X_p = 0$ is given by $\left| \boldsymbol{n} \cdot x_i + \left(\frac{\beta_0}{\|\beta\|} \right) \right| = \left| \frac{1}{\|\beta\|} (\beta_1 x_{i1} + \cdots + \beta_p x_{ip}) + \frac{\beta_0}{\|\beta\|} \right|$

$$= \left| \frac{\beta_0 + \beta_1 x_{i1} + \cdots + \beta_p x_{ip}}{\|\beta\|} \right|$$

$$= \frac{1}{\|\beta\|} \left| \beta_0 + \beta_1 x_{i1} + \cdots + \beta_p x_{ip} \right|$$

$$= \frac{1}{\|\beta\|} \begin{cases} \beta_0 + \beta_1 x_{i1} + \cdots + \beta_p x_{ip}, & \text{if } \beta_0 + \beta_1 x_{i1} + \cdots + \beta_p x_{ip} > 0 \\ -(\beta_0 + \beta_1 x_{i1} + \cdots + \beta_p x_{ip}), & \text{if } \beta_0 + \beta_1 x_{i1} + \cdots + \beta_p x_{ip} < 0 \end{cases}$$

$$= \frac{1}{\|\beta\|} \begin{cases} \beta_0 + \beta_1 x_{i1} + \cdots + \beta_p x_{ip}, & \text{if } y_i = 1 \\ -(\beta_0 + \beta_1 x_{i1} + \cdots + \beta_p x_{ip}), & \text{if } y_i = -1 \end{cases}$$

$$= \frac{1}{\|\beta\|} y_i (\beta_0 + \beta_1 x_{i1} + \cdots + \beta_p x_{ip})$$

Hence, the perpendicular distance between x_i and the separating hyperplane $\beta_0 + \beta_1 X_1 + \cdots + \beta_p X_p = 0$ is given by $\frac{1}{\|\beta\|} y_i (\beta_0 + \beta_1 x_{i1} + \cdots + \beta_p x_{ip})$.

APPENDIX 2

Claim: For any positive scalar k, $M_{k\beta_0, k\beta} = M_{\beta_0, \beta}$.

Proof: $M_{k\beta_0, k\beta} = min\left\{\frac{1}{k\|\beta\|} y_i\left(k\beta_0 + k\beta_1 x_{i1} + \cdots + k\beta_p x_{ip}\right) | i = 1, \ldots, N\right\}$

$= min\left\{\frac{k}{k\|\beta\|} y_i\left(\beta_0 + \beta_1 x_{i1} + \cdots + \beta_p x_{ip}\right) | i = 1, \ldots, N\right\}$

$= min\left\{\frac{1}{\|\beta\|} y_i\left(\beta_0 + \beta_1 x_{i1} + \cdots + \beta_p x_{ip}\right) | i = 1, \ldots, N\right\}$

$= M_{\beta_0, \beta}$

APPENDIX 3

Claim: The problem $\underset{(\beta_0,\beta)\in S}{maximize}\ M_{\beta_0,\beta}$ is equivalent to the problem

$\underset{(\beta_0,\beta)\in S}{maximize}\ M_{\beta_0,\beta}$ given the constraint $\min\{y_i(\beta_0 + \cdots + \beta_p x_{ip})|i = 1, \dots, N\} = 1$.

('Equivalent' here means that the first problem has a solution if and only if the second problem has a solution.)

Proof: Suppose $(\beta_0^*, \beta_1^*, \dots, \beta_p^*) \in S$ is a solution to $\underset{(\beta_0,\beta)\in S}{maximize}\ M_{\beta_0,\beta}$. We will scale the beta's to get a solution to $\underset{(\beta_0,\beta)\in S}{maximize}\ M_{\beta_0,\beta}$ given the constraint $\min\{y_i(\beta_0 + \cdots + \beta_p x_{ip})|i = 1, \dots, N\} = 1$.

We can scale our $\beta's$ by $k = \dfrac{1}{\|\beta^*\| M_{\beta_0^*,\beta^*}}$ to get a solution that has the same maximum $M_{\beta_0^*,\beta^*}$ and satisfies the condition $\min\{y_i(\beta_0 + \cdots + \beta_p x_{ip})|i = 1, \dots, N\} = 1$.

$$\min\{y_i(k\beta_0^* + k\beta_1^* x_{i1} + \cdots + k\beta_p^* x_{ip})|i = 1, \dots, N\}$$

$$= k \min\{y_i(\beta_0^* + \beta_1^* x_{i1} + \cdots + \beta_p^* x_{ip})|i = 1, \dots, N\}$$

$$= k\|\beta^*\| M_{\beta_0^*,\beta^*}$$

$$= \frac{1}{\|\beta^*\| M_{\beta_0^*,\beta^*}} \cdot \|\beta^*\| M_{\beta_0^*,\beta^*}$$

$$= 1.$$

So $(k\beta_0^*, k\beta_1^*, \dots, k\beta_p^*)$ satisfies the constraint. We also know that $(k\beta_0^*, k\beta_1^*, \dots, k\beta_p^*)$ maximizes $M_{\beta_0,\beta}$ over all elements in S that satisfy the constraint because $M_{k\beta_0^*,k\beta^*} = M_{\beta_0^*,\beta^*} \geq M_{\beta_0,\beta}$ for all $(\beta_0,\beta) \in S$ that satisfy the constraint. Therefore, $(k\beta_0^*, k\beta_1^*, \dots, k\beta_p^*)$ is a solution to

$\underset{(\beta_0,\beta)\in S}{maximize}\ M_{\beta_0,\beta}$ given the constraint $\min\{y_i(\beta_0 + \cdots + \beta_p x_{ip})|i = 1, \dots, N\} = 1$.

Now, suppose (β_0^+, β^+) is a solution to

$\underset{(\beta_0,\beta)\in S}{maximize}\ M_{\beta_0,\beta}$ given the constraint $\min\{y_i(\beta_0 + \cdots + \beta_p x_{ip})|i = 1, \dots, N\} = 1$.

We'll show that (β_0^+, β^+) is a solution to $\underset{(\beta_0,\beta)\in S}{maximize}\ M_{\beta_0,\beta}$. We need to show $M_{\beta_0^+,\beta^+} \geq M_{\beta_0,\beta}\ \forall (\beta_0,\beta) \in S$.

Let $(\beta_0,\beta) \in S$. Let $k = \dfrac{1}{\|\beta\| M_{\beta_0,\beta}}$.

$\Rightarrow (k\beta_0, k\beta)$ satisfies $\min\{y_i(\beta_0 + \cdots + \beta_p x_{ip})|i = 1, \dots, N\} = 1$

$\Rightarrow M_{\beta_0^+,\beta^+} \geq M_{k\beta_0,k\beta}$ because (β_0^+, β^+) is a solution to the constrained problem

$$\Rightarrow \quad M_{\beta_0^+,\beta^+} \geq M_{\beta_0,\beta} \quad \text{since } M_{k\beta_0,k\beta} = M_{\beta_0,\beta}$$

APPENDIX 4

Let the following problems be called (1) and (2):

(1) $\underset{(\beta_0,\beta)\in S}{minimize}$ $\frac{1}{2}\|\beta\|^2$ given the constraint $\min\{y_i(\beta_0 + \cdots + \beta_p x_{ip})|i = 1, ..., N\} = 1$

(2) $\underset{(\beta_0,\beta)\in S}{minimize}$ $\frac{1}{2}\|\beta\|^2$ given the constraint $\min\{y_i(\beta_0 + \cdots + \beta_p x_{ip})|i = 1, ..., N\} \geq 1$

Claim: Problem (1) is equivalent to problem (2).

Proof: Suppose $(\beta_0^+, \beta^+) \in S$ is a solution to (2).

Let $k = \dfrac{1}{\|\beta^+\|M_{\beta_0^+,\beta^+}}$.

Then $\min\{y_i(k\beta_0^+ + \cdots + k\beta_p^+ x_{ip})|i = 1, ..., N\}$

$= k \min\{y_i(\beta_0^+ + \cdots + \beta_p^+ x_{ip})|i = 1, ..., N\}$

$= \dfrac{1}{\|\beta^+\|M_{\beta_0^+,\beta^+}} \cdot \|\beta^+\|M_{\beta_0^+,\beta^+}$

$= 1.$

Let $(\beta_0, \beta) \in S$ such that $\min\{y_i(\beta_0 + \cdots + \beta_p x_{ip})|i = 1, ..., N\} = 1$

$\Rightarrow \min\{y_i(\beta_0 + \cdots + \beta_p x_{ip})|i = 1, ..., N\} \geq 1$

$\Rightarrow \frac{1}{2}\|\beta^+\|^2 \leq \frac{1}{2}\|\beta\|^2$

Now,

$$\frac{1}{2}\|k\beta^+\|^2 = \frac{1}{2}k^2\|\beta^+\|^2 = \frac{1}{2}\frac{1}{(M_{\beta_0^+,\beta^+})^2\|\beta^+\|^2}\|\beta^+\|^2 = \frac{1}{2}\frac{1}{(M_{\beta_0^+,\beta^+})^2}$$

$$= \frac{1}{2}\frac{1}{\frac{1}{\|\beta^+\|^2}\min\{y_i(\beta_0^+ + \cdots + \beta_p^+ x_{ip})|i = 1, ..., N\}^2}$$

$$= \frac{1}{2}\frac{\|\beta^+\|^2}{\min\{y_i(\beta_0^+ + \cdots + \beta_p^+ x_{ip})|i = 1, ..., N\}^2}$$

$\leq \frac{1}{2}\|\beta^+\|^2$ because $\min\{y_i(\beta_0^+ + \cdots + \beta_p^+ x_{ip})|i = 1, ..., N\} \geq 1$

$\leq \frac{1}{2}\|\beta\|^2$ because we showed $\frac{1}{2}\|\beta^+\|^2 \leq \frac{1}{2}\|\beta\|^2$ earlier.

$\Rightarrow (k\beta_0^+, k\beta^+)$ is a solution to (1).

Now we show the equivalence in the other direction.

Suppose $(\beta_0^*, \beta^*) \in S$ is a solution to (1).

Let $(\beta_0, \beta) \in S$ such that $\min\{y_i(\beta_0 + \cdots + \beta_p x_{ip})|i = 1, \ldots, N\} \geq 1$.

Let $k = \frac{1}{M_{\beta_0,\beta}\|\beta\|}$. Then $\min\{y_i(k\beta_0 + \cdots + k\beta_p x_{ip})|i = 1, \ldots, N\}$

$$= k \; \min\{y_i(\beta_0 + \cdots + \beta_p x_{ip})|i = 1, \ldots, N\}$$

$$= \frac{1}{M_{\beta_0,\beta}\|\beta\|} \cdot M_{\beta_0,\beta}\|\beta\|$$

$$= 1.$$

$$\Rightarrow \tfrac{1}{2}\|\beta^*\|^2 \leq \tfrac{1}{2}\|k\beta\|^2 \quad \text{because } (\beta_0^*, \beta^*) \text{ is a solution to (1)}$$

Now, $\frac{1}{2}\|k\beta\|^2 = \frac{1}{2}k^2\|\beta\|^2$

$$= \frac{1}{2}\frac{1}{M_{\beta_0,\beta}^2\|\beta\|^2}\|\beta\|^2$$

$$= \frac{1}{2}\frac{1}{M_{\beta_0,\beta}^2}$$

$$= \frac{1}{2}\frac{1}{\frac{1}{\|\beta\|^2}\min\{y_i(\beta_0 + \cdots + \beta_p \, x_{ip})|i = 1, \ldots, N\}^2}$$

$$= \frac{1}{2}\frac{\|\beta\|^2}{\min\{y_i(\beta_0 + \cdots + \beta_p \, x_{ip})|i = 1, \ldots, N\}^2}$$

$$\leq \tfrac{1}{2}\|\beta\|^2 \quad \text{because } (\beta_0, \beta) \text{ satisfies } \min\{y_i(\beta_0 + \cdots + \beta_p x_{ip})|i = 1, \ldots, N\} \geq 1$$

So $\frac{1}{2}\|\beta^*\|^2 \leq \frac{1}{2}\|k\beta\|^2 \leq \frac{1}{2}\|\beta\|^2$

$$\Rightarrow \tfrac{1}{2}\|\beta^*\|^2 \leq \tfrac{1}{2}\|\beta\|^2$$

$$\Rightarrow (\beta_0^*, \beta^*) \text{ is a solution to (2).}$$

APPENDIX 5

Let the following problems be called (1) and (2):

(1) $\underset{(\beta_0,\beta)\in S}{minimize}$ $\frac{1}{2}\|\beta\|^2$ given the constraint $\min\{y_i(\beta_0 + \cdots + \beta_p x_{ip})|i = 1, ..., N\} = 1$

(2) $\underset{(\beta_0,\beta)\in S}{maximize}$ $\frac{1}{2}\|\beta\|^2$ given the constraint $\min\{y_i(\beta_0 + \cdots + \beta_p x_{ip})|i = 1, ..., N\} \geq 1$

Claim: The solutions to problems (1) and (2) give the same maximum values.

Proof: Suppose $(\beta_0^+, \beta^+) \in S$ is a solution to (2) and $(\beta_0^*, \beta^*) \in S$ is a solution to (1).

Then, $\frac{1}{2}\|\beta^+\|^2 \leq \frac{1}{2}\|\beta^*\|^2$ because (β_0^*, β^*) satisfies the constraint
$\min\{y_i(\beta_0 + \cdots + \beta_p x_{ip})|i = 1, ..., N\} = 1$ and hence the constraint
$\min\{y_i(\beta_0 + \cdots + \beta_p x_{ip})|i = 1, ..., N\} \geq 1$, and (β_0^+, β^+) minimizes
$\frac{1}{2}\|\beta\|^2$ over all such (β_0, β).

$\Rightarrow \quad \|\beta^+\| \leq \|\beta^*\|$

$\Rightarrow \quad \|\beta^+\| \leq \frac{1}{M_{\beta_0^*,\beta^*}}$ because $M_{\beta_0^*,\beta^*} = \frac{1}{\|\beta^*\|}$.

However, $M_{\beta_0^+,\beta^+} = \frac{1}{\|\beta^+\|}\min\{y_i(\beta_0^+ + \cdots + \beta_p^+ x_{ip})|i = 1, ..., N\}$

$\geq \frac{1}{\|\beta^+\|}$.

So $\|\beta^+\| \geq \frac{1}{M_{\beta_0^+,\beta^+}}$.

It follows that $\frac{1}{M_{\beta_0^+,\beta^+}} \leq \|\beta^+\| \leq \frac{1}{M_{\beta_0^*,\beta^*}}$

$\Rightarrow \quad M_{\beta_0^*,\beta^*} \leq M_{\beta_0^+,\beta^+}.$

Note that (β_0^*, β^*) is a solution to (1) and hence a solution to

$\underset{(\beta_0,\beta)\in S}{maximize}$ $M_{\beta_0,\beta}$ given the constraint $\min\{y_i(\beta_0 + \cdots + \beta_p x_{ip})|i = 1, ..., N\} = 1.$

We showed earlier that a solution to

$\underset{(\beta_0,\beta)\in S}{maximize}$ $M_{\beta_0,\beta}$ given the constraint $\min\{y_i(\beta_0 + \cdots + \beta_p x_{ip})|i = 1, ..., N\} = 1$

is also a solution to the original maximization problem $\underset{(\beta_0,\beta)\in S}{maximize}$ $M_{\beta_0,\beta}$.

So (β_0^*, β^*) is a solution to $\underset{(\beta_0, \beta) \in S}{maximize} \; M_{\beta_0, \beta}$.

$\implies M_{\beta_0^*, \beta^*} \geq M_{\beta_0, \beta}$ for any $(\beta_0, \beta) \in S$.

In particular, $M_{\beta_0^*, \beta^*} \geq M_{\beta_0^+, \beta^+}$.

$\implies M_{\beta_0^*, \beta^*} \leq M_{\beta_0^+, \beta^+} \leq M_{\beta_0^*, \beta^*}$

$\implies M_{\beta_0^*, \beta^*} = M_{\beta_0^+, \beta^+}$.

Thus, the solutions to (1) and (2) give the same maximum values.

INDEX

Made in the USA
Lexington, KY
21 September 2018